GRUMPY OLD MEN

GRUMPY

A Manual for

DAVID QUANTICK

OLD MEN

the British Malcontent

HarperCollins*Publishers*

First published in Great Britain in 2004
by HarperCollins*Entertainment*
an imprint of HarperCollins*Publishers* London

Copyright © David Quantick 2004

2

A CIP catalogue record for this book
is available from the British Library

The HarperCollins website address is: www.harpercollins.co.uk

ISBN 0-00-718993-1

Printed and bound in Great Britain by Clays Ltd, St Ives plc

ACKNOWLEDGEMENTS

THE PART OF A BOOK WHERE SOMEONE YOU DON'T GIVE A TOSS ABOUT THANKS A LOAD OF PEOPLE YOU'VE NEVER HEARD OF BUT WHO HE PROBABLY OWES MONEY OR DRUGS.

WITH THAT IN MIND, THANKS TO THE GRUMPY OLD MEN OF ALL AGES WHO'VE CONTRIBUTED THEIR TALES OF WOE TO THIS BOOK.

THANKS ALSO TO JON NAISMITH FOR MAKING ME EDIT BITS THAT I PERSONALLY THOUGHT WERE FINE IN THE FIRST PLACE AND TO KATE HALDANE FOR MAKING ME DO IT WHEN I COULD HAVE BEEN ASLEEP IN A NICE WARM GUTTER.

CONTENTS
~

INTRODUCTION

A recent survey – no wait! come back! – a recent survey indicated that the grumpiest people in Britain are men aged between 35 and 54. Not, as you might think, proper old people with creaking joints and memories of when it was all fields round here.

Today's grumpy old men are not just the older generation. We're not all going round acting like extras from Dad's Army, whingeing around on the seafront moaning about the Hun. No, today's grumpy old men, like policemen and Sting, are getting younger every day. We know the difference between CD and DVD, we remember when 'boy bands' meant The Sex Pistols and The Clash, and we dress more like our sons than our dads. Today's grumpy old men are stuck between devil-may-care youth and past-all-caring old age, griping and groaning and generally having a miserable time.

It doesn't help that we're British, either. Looking around at our international neighbours, we Brits do seem to be a lot grumpier than them. Whoever even heard of a sulky Spaniard? A bad-tempered Dutchman? A cranky Italian (well, apart from Mussolini). Even the French are less irritable than we are, and that's saying a lot. But cross the English Channel and you are in a land of grump.

Some facts and figures: 36% of us can't even afford a week's holiday away from home, compared with 12% in Germany, France and the Netherlands. This is probably because we live on a big wet rock, or 'island', whereas people in Germany, France and the Netherlands just have to step outside the front door and hey presto! they are in the Netherlands, Germany or France.

The weather here is shocking. It rains in summer, it snows in spring, it floods in autumn and it's unspeakable in winter. Living in Britain is like living in a cold swamp. Foreigners notice that we talk about the weather quite a lot. And we do, nervously, as the people of a village terrorised by a wolf or a serial killer might.

Also there's not much room in here. There are 78 people per square kilometre in Spain, 106 in France – and 243 in the United Kingdom. 243 people per square kilometre! Never mind enough room to swing a cat, that's not enough room to frisk a cockroach. And it is us British men who get the worst of it.

Scientists working in science labs in Edinburgh – real scientists, with leather elbow patches – have identified what they call 'Irritable Male Syndrome', caused by sinking testosterone levels. IMS affects 30% of all men – that's all men, not just Old Man Steptoe – and manifests itself in the following ways: depression, loss of energy, low self-esteem, reduced libido and… irritability. Doctor Christopher Steidle, an eminent urologist (now there's a job to make you grumpy), says, 'Many of the symptoms are indistinguishable from old age, and for years you've always thought of it as "grumpy old man" syndrome. Now we know what the grumpy old man probably has.'

So what, as we all become grumpy old men, does this mean for the future? This. As our testosterone levels go off to join the dodo, the passenger pigeon and decent plays on BBC1, it is going to get more and more rubbish being a man these days. Sexual equality in relationships means we can no longer roll home drunk at lunchtime and expect a roast dinner and all the ironing done. Erosion of the traditional family means that kids grow up faster and therefore notice what prats their dads are at an earlier age. This in turn is worsened by a tide of new technologies which leaves many of us feeling like Piltdown Man on a stupid day. We're supposed to be the ones who tell kids how to work machinery, but these days only the under-tens know how to reconfigure a computer, plug in a PlayStation, or upload into an mp3 player.

Add to this mixture the fact that if you're aged between 35 and 54, you're too old to be running round high on alcopops, and too young

to be cheating at dominoes in the snug. The results are clear: the new generation of grumpy old men is caught in a cleft stick of general lifey crapness.

This book is written by grumpy old men for grumpy old men. It asks ageless questions like 'What's the point?' and 'When will it

stop?' and answers them as unreasonably and bad-temperedly as possible. We can't make it better but we can shout at it and spoil its day. This book exists to put the 'rant' in 'intolerant' and the 'bastard' into 'go to hell, you bastard'.

Read it, and cease to weep.

ENTERTAINMENT

*'This is what we mean by a theme pub: a pub which used to be
normal but was turned into some kind of museum of twit crap.'*

CINEMAS
~

Evil places. They used to be huge, and now they are tiny. This is so
they can cram billions more people in, and also means the screen is
so small that people think they're watching the telly with 75 strangers.

Cinemas are tolerable in the dark, but turn the light on and
urghhh... the floor is strewn with trodden-in food, sticky with split
soft drinks, and a death trap for people liable to slipping on popcorn.
And the people! Half of them are mouth-breathing illiterates who
laugh at jokes some ten minutes after the joke has been told, who
explain the movie's simple plot to their even simpler friends and who
think that, somewhere on the film certificate they show as the movie
starts, it says, 'Please start talking in a loud voice now.' The other half
are *Guardian*-reading ponces who go to arty movies and laugh loudly
at any feeble joke to show they get French humour. Somehow they
are worse, possibly because they smell of carrot cake.

At least that's something in favour of normal cinemas. They don't
sell carrot cake. They couldn't, it's too small. Normal cinemas only
sell gargantuan food and drink, as though they're expecting a party
of ogres to come in and see *Finding Nemo*. The soft drinks are the
size of nuclear power station cooling tanks (and just as radioactive).
The popcorn looks like the grain harvest of a small Asian nation.
And the sweets – a cinema-sized bag of wine gums is the size, weight
and colour of a psychedelic sack of coal.

The reason the food crap and drink crap are so large is an obvious one; so they can charge more. A table for two at the Savoy Grill, with both of you drinking champagne by the vat, and having cigars after, and some caviar in a bap, would be cheaper than going to a cinema and having a large coke and plate of 'nachos' (old library tickets boiled in cornmeal).

MOVIE TRAILERS

1) AND NOW! – A HEARTWARMING STORY OF TWO GENERATIONS! Wow! Thanks for the warning! Let's make a really big mental note not to see that film.

2) Those are the best 30 seconds in the movie? They must be, if that's what they used for the trailer. How the hell bad are the other three hours 29 minutes and 30 seconds?

3) Didn't we see this trailer last week?

4) And aren't we going to see it on every DVD that we rent?

5) Well, that was the entire plot of the film. Hardly worth going to see it now.

HAIR ADS
≈

Wash your hair with this chemical gloop – which we've called oxycortiferogerontizine although you will know it better as 'donkey widdle' – and it'll have more 'body'. Later it will fall out, giving your carpet more 'body'. Hair ads are the only places left, apart from crack dens, where you can still boast about how many chemicals you've put in something.

And who are all these scientists in science labs, working day and night to invent shinier hair? No wonder there isn't a cure for the common cold. 'Sorry Mrs Smith, your husband is going to die of Lassa fever but good news! We've cleared up his dandruff.'

PERFUME ADS
≈

What in the name of hell are you talking about? What's that woman doing? Why is everyone mumbling in a French accent? Where are your trousers? Is that a plinth? What's happened to the furniture?

Perfume ads may not tell you anything about the product they're selling, but they do accurately describe the state of your mind if you drink some.

LOAN ADS
≈

Only worthless TV presenter scum front these ads. Who else but a fourth-rate talking head who isn't doing that well would think it a good idea to sell crippling loans to members of the public with bad credit records? The near-equivalent of actual conmen, loan ad presenters are inches away from being criminals. They are saying, 'I am famous so take my advice and get more into debt than you were before.' Vile grinning filth. See also 'Have you been hurt in a trip or fall?' You'll be hurt in a fall in a minute, you ambulance-chasing ghoul. Get something bad and die.

BOOZE ADS
∾

These stupid ads are always set in glittering bars and discos, where the occupants are all in their 20s and have been going at the liquor like billy-o. They are always laughing and dancing and shaking bottles so the contents go everywhere. A real bar full of pissed-up 20-year-olds would be hell on earth. What these ads don't show is that ten minutes after the camera crew left, a huge fist-fight broke out and one of the male models smashed an empty rum bottle and tried to glass the other male model.

'IRISH' PUBS
∾

Ever been to Ireland? Some of the pubs are lovely, but a lot of them are, in fact, concrete sheds that smell of damp and bad furniture. Lots of them look like quiet British country pubs. Quite a

few are modern and trendy with lots of shiny metal. And until recently very few of them had any of the following in them:

1) *Vintage Guinness posters*

2) *Old road signs saying DUBLIN 43 MILES*

3) *Green neon signs in the shape of shamrocks*

4) *Lager*

5) *2 different kinds of Irish whiskey*

6) *A jukebox stacked with the complete works of The Pogues (from London) and The Waterboys (from Scotland)*

7) *The entire contents of a provincial Irish grocer's shop or sub post office, circa 1956*

8) *A signed photograph of U2*

9) *A lunch menu that offers a choice of soda bread or mussels*

10) *Toilets with signs in Gaelic*

And yet this is the old toot that passes for Irish authenticity in your average faux Irish pub. Around the world, from Chile to Moscow, from Nepal to Tierra Del Fuego, the fake Irish bar has spread, along with all the other vexing drivel of fake Paddywhackery. Designed to appeal to the same kind of cultural illiterate who thinks Scotland is in Wales, the Faux Irish bar is like some sick prop out of a brewer's idea of Westworld, where animatronic farm labourers drink CGI pints of Guinness and sing The Men Behind The Wire to an mp3 accompaniment of Uilleann pipes and bodhrans.

Still, we should be grateful that the world's most popular theme bar is not the 'Essex Pub'. Dear God.

THE THEATRE

'The only thing I get from the theatre,' Paul McCartney said to Joe Orton, 'is a sore arse.' While this was a remark that Orton relished on several levels, it does have the force of truth behind it. Theatres are rubbish. In other cultures, theatre is acknowledged to be historically and ethnically an important part of a nation's cultural past. In ours, we still let actors, directors and critics pretend that it's important. It's not; it's a leftover art form from the olden days that's about as relevant to the times as operetta, the York Mystery Plays and Morris Dancing. And a lot less enjoyable.

Where do we begin to tell the story of how crap a night at the theatre can be? For a start, most old theatres are the size of a kennel. Theatre designers spent so much time on the rococo balustrades and filigree

And then they want you to buy a programme. This is a piece of cheaply printed tat which looks a bit like a football programme but is spectacularly more dull.

whatnottery that they obviously forgot to put the seats in. The foyer is designed to prevent any swinging of cats. And the Royal Box is, literally, a box.

And then they want you to buy a programme. This is a piece of cheaply printed tat which looks a bit like a football programme but is spectacularly more dull. A theatre programme contains the following rotten items:

1) *A history of the play, which, had you read it before you booked the tickets, would have caused you to never set foot in a theatre again.*

2) *A biography of the director, who comes over as a cross between Rommel and a halfwit.*

3) *The actual 'programme', which claims that Act 1 takes place in some git's front room, and Act 2 in the same git's front room, 'several years later'. This tells you nothing, except that you have spent £50 to spend five hours looking at the same eight pieces of flyblown scenery.*

4) *A biography of the leading lady, who seems to have alternated her career between playing Shakespearian heroines and appearing in* Crossroads.

5) *A biography of the leading man, who, reading between the lines, appears to have been too pissed to work for most of his career.*

6) *An advert on the back for* Cats.

This piece of old toot will set you back ten quid. It will take you 20 minutes to read, not because it's interesting, because it isn't interesting, but because the print is so small. This will however kill time during the interval. Do not under any circumstances go to the bar during the interval, even if you have 'pre-ordered' your drinks. There is one barman, five hundred booze-craving punters and the bar is the size of a pencil case.

DVDS
~

The new visual format, but just as annoying as the old ones. For a start, they're more expensive. Then half the time you're just buying a movie you bought in 1995 on video because of the 'improved picture quality', which isn't improved because the DVD manufacturer copied it off the same 1995 video.

Ah, but what about the DVD extras? Yes. What about them? DVD extras, when attached to a bad movie, are like all the trimmings to an excellent roast dinner without any actual meat. There's the Audio Commentary, which is three actors and the director meeting up two years later and trying to think of something interesting to say about this awful film they made.

CREDITS ROLL: WE SEE A BEAUTIFUL NEW HAMPSHIRE SUNRISE

DIRECTOR'S VOICE

Ah... hi... and... ah... welcome to the audio commentary to *Autumn Of My Life*. I'm the director, Hal Franklin, and I'm joined by the giggly actress who played the lead, Francine Mehitabel, and a stupid young guy who played her simpleton brother, Alistair Tug.

GIGGLY ACTRESS
Hi!

STUPID YOUNG GUY
Yeah. What she said.

THE SUNRISE IS REPLACED BY A SHOT OF A RIVER

DIRECTOR
Yeah, this is, ah, the opening, ah, shot of the movie. I remember
we scouted for months to find the right river. We must have been
to over 40 states, and finally! we found this river right on our
doorstep.

GIGGLY ACTRESS
I fell in the river!

STUPID YOUNG GUY
Yeah! That was funny!

And so on until you either run screaming from the room or rip the
plug out of the machine and throw it into the street. This is the only
good DVD commentary:

CREDITS ROLL: A BEAUTIFUL NEW HAMPSHIRE SUNRISE

DIRECTOR'S VOICE
Hi, and welcome to the audio commentary to *Autumn Of My Life*.
I'm the director, Hal Franklin, and I'm joined by the film's stars,
Francine Mehitabel and Alistair Tug.

FRANCINE AND ALISTAIR
Hi!

DIRECTOR
And we're also joined by a ravenous man-eating tiger.

TIGER
Grrr! Bite! Kill! Etc.

Much better. And that's just Disc One.

PLAYS

～

There are five kinds of play:

1) SHAKESPEARE. Updated or traditional, Shakespeare is always done in a stupid, rhymey voice that just looks weird now. You know all the good bits already and the rest is a bit hard to understand. And no way are the comedy bits ever funny.

2) FARCE. Farce is either French, which means maids and Poirot moustaches, or English, which means vicars and double meanings. Either way, it relies completely on some tit leaving the room or hiding just as another tit comes in. No farce would ever work in a desert. 'Hello, there's Eric. You've got no trousers on, Eric.' 'Yes, sorry about that, I've been having sex with your wife.'

3) IBSEN, CHEKHOV, ETC. Oh Lord. We're all going to die! Can we start with the people on stage first, please?

4) OSCAR WILDE. Again, you know all the jokes, the plots are unconvincing, the younger members of the cast don't understand any of the play, and everyone just wants to hear the old theatre dame say, 'A haaaandbag!' in a silly voice.

5) FILMS TURNED INTO PLAYS WITH SOMEONE WHO USED TO BE IN AN AMERICAN SITCOM IN THEM. Like watching a film acted out on a stage very slowly with someone who used to be in an American sitcom shouting their heads off. Later, a middle-aged lady who was in a film once will take her top off.

ROCK MUSICALS

～

Rock musicals were once very different from today's rock musicals as they featured original songs and were like your mum's idea of rock music, i.e. opera songs done loudly by hairy stage school students with lots of guitar solos at the wrong moment. Most, for some reason, were set in Biblical times and conspired to give the impression that Jesus was a hippy and the Disciples were drug addicts.

Now 'rock musicals' are something else entirely. They are made up

of bits of old rock songs and plots that wouldn't fool a kitten. Abba musicals, Madness musicals, Buddy Holly musicals, Queen musicals and even Rod Stewart musicals. Recycling proper rock songs and getting stage-school johnnies to sing them in castrated voices with good diction is hugely popular, and coachloads of people come in to hear music they loved as teenagers kicked in the arse by dancing gimps.

Soon people will only form bands so that a rock musical will be based on their songs. Soon people will only know the work of, say, Bob Dylan from the new West End show, *It's All Right Ma, I'm Only Singing And Dancing*. The Sex Pistols will be commemorated by Ben Elton's latest masterpiece, *We're So Pretty, Mister Vacant*. And anyone who fancies a nostalgic evening sound-tracked by the music of Kraftwerk can go and see *Autobahn!* at the Leeds City Varieties, with Jane McDonald as The Model and Darren Day as Trans-Europe Express the Singing Train.

THEME PUBS
∾

Pub. There's a word. It's short for 'public house', you know. And therein lies a clue. Pubs aren't bars, they aren't inns, they're not roadhouses or gin palaces or after-hours clubs, they're public houses. Which means that, while they are indeed open to the public and a jolly good thing too, they are also, in a way, sort of, houses. Rundown houses, admittedly, that smell of fags and have a slightly sticky carpet. Houses that might belong to someone who does drink a lot but has got it under control, but houses. Because the best pubs are a bit like a little home from home. There might be a fireplace. There will be people you know. The landlord and bar staff will make you feel like a welcome guest. If there is a jukebox, it will confine itself entirely to singles and albums you own yourself, with particular reference to records you bought between the ages of 15 and 25. It will be warm. It will not be enormous. And it will be a pleasant place to spend the evening with friends. Oh, and there might be a big black hairy dog that likes crisps.

What it will NOT be is a theme pub. Theme pubs are, as their stupid name suggests, pubs laid out according to a (do you see?) theme. Now traditionally, in a way, all pubs are theme pubs. Their theme is Beer. Some pubs have slightly more developed themes like 'The Landlord Was In The Navy' or 'We Collect Dirty Crinkled Foreign Banknotes And Stick Them On The Wall'. Other pubs are unintentionally themed, like 'Pub Full Of Cockney Murderers' or 'Pub Where They Play A Bit Too Many Goth CDs'. But these are not what we mean by theme pubs.

This is what we mean by a theme pub: a pub which used to be normal but was turned, at great expense and for no real reason, into some kind of museum of twit crap. Thus the Bird In Hand might be gutted, remade and remodelled into Graceland, an Elvis Presley-themed pub. Where once there was a duff painting of a dog looking askance at a pheasant, now there is a white neon guitar with ELVIS written on it. Where there used to be some weird old bits of broken farm equipment, there is a sequinned satin jumpsuit in a glass case. And where the jukebox would occasionally deafen punters with random selections from Thin Lizzy's *Live And Dangerous*, now all it plays is DJ remixes of bad Elvis singles. Oh, and the beer is some sort of bottled ant sweat with a Confederate flag on the label that no-one in America has ever heard of. The bar staff are suicidal and the clientele is that delightful mixture of bewildered tourists and recently-released serial killers. But it is a Theme Pub and as such looks good in the brewery's free magazine.

> Oh, and the beer is some sort of bottled ant sweat with a Confederate flag on the label that no-one in America has ever heard of.

ANIMALS

'If cats could find a way to push all the people in the world into an active volcano and still open all the tins of catfood, they would.'

CATS

～

Cats are bastards. There it is in cold print. Cats are bastards. If a cat was a man, it would let you buy it beer all night and then have sex with your girlfriend. If a cat was a criminal (and, oh, it is), it would leave you to do whatever the hard part of a bank robbery was, and then, when you were doing that thing with the safe and the stethoscope, run away with all the money and tell the police you did it. If cats were lifeguards (and they're not, because cats are scared of water the way vampires are scared of sunlight – coincidence? No), they'd sit there on their wooden lighthouse towers with their cat legs crossed watching as people drowned in the ocean. Cats are, in short, the scum of the earth.

Here's a clue about cats: tigers. Are tigers bastards? Yes. And what are tigers? Just big cats. Therefore cats are tigers only smaller. Therefore they are bastards. Here's another clue. Lions. What do lions do? Lie around all day and then, when they're bored, jump a giraffe and eat it. Cats don't even do that. Ever see a cat jump a giraffe? No. Why? Because we've cossetted them and welcomed them into our homes and invented catfood, just for them the idle bastards.

Hey! When you're sitting in the front room watching the telly and the cat comes in with a dead bird in its mouth, or kicking a half-alive mouse down the carpet, and some visiting idiot says, 'Ah look, he's brought you a present,' they're wrong. Cats do not bring people presents, the same as they don't buy flowers or offer to help out with

the rent. Cats don't give a toss about people. If cats could find a way to push all the people in the world into an active volcano and still open all the tins of catfood, they would. So why is the cat bringing you a dead sparrow or mouse? Because they want you to cook it for them, that's why. And while you're at it, maybe make them a pair of mouseskin trousers and a fetching little hat, with some sparrow feathers on the brim. Bastards.

Another thing about cats which is false is the fool remark that they're intelligent. Now this might wash to some extent with dolphins, who do seem to talk a bit and can do tricks but cats? Come off it. Here's a simple test; lock the cat in the house, having first blocked up the catflap. Put a chair next to the keyhole for the back door and on that chair place the key to the back door. Tell the cat, in short words, that the key on the chair will open the back door. And go to Florida for six months (using the front door). When you come back, will you find a) the back door opened and all your possessions removed and sold, b) an armed gang of felines waiting for you to exact a terrible revenge, or c) the skeleton of a cat? Case rested or what? Bugger off, cats and take ocelots with you.

SQUIRRELS
∾

Red squirrels. How we loved them, with their cute ears and their little faces and their russet fur. We even, bafflingly, based a road safety campaign around a red squirrel. These days, if they wanted to find Tufty to interview him on one of those nostalgia TV shows, they'd be stuffed. Tufty has gone the way of all flesh, driven out of his native Nutwood City Limits or wherever he lived by a grey squirrel, name of Arseface. What was the deal with red squirrels, that they wouldn't stand up and fight for their red squirrel rights? Were they too busy hoarding acorns for the long winter, or were they just too interested in learning about road safety? Either way, the grey squirrels moved in and trashed the neighbourhood.

Grey squirrels – someone called them 'jazz rats', a rare combination of two unpopular things. Grey squirrels are the cuckoos of the squirrel world and they should be outed as such. Just pray that one day, what with genetic engineering, GM foods, global warming and all, it's just a matter of time until the big mauve squirrels come along and give the grey squirrels the kicking they so richly deserve.

WASPS
∾

What's the point of wasps? We've got mosquitos and we've got bees and we really don't need some inbetweeny stripey stinging spiv as well. Wasps are crap. The only reason Noah took two wasps onto the Ark was they probably stung the unicorns to death and nicked their tickets. That's the kind of useful animal wasps are.

Wasps are, in fact, bees gone bad. Not literally, obviously, nobody really thinks that if a bee is naughty, it starts smoking tabs and building a paper nest. Wasps resemble bees in many ways; they buzz, they're stripey, they have queens, and that's it. Wasps are sods. At school they probably bullied the bees and made them do their homework for them. Later they would go out drinking with a bee because the bee had a car, and then the wasps would rob a sub post office and make the bee take the rap. Wasps are not bees. There's no kids' book about a wasp being friends with an ant because wasps don't have friends. Ha ha! Look at the lonely wasp!

The real difference between bees and wasps is this; when a bee stings you, it dies. Its only weapon, other than pollen, is fatal to it. When a wasp stings you, it doesn't die. It just laughs and twirls its imaginary moustache.

> When a wasp stings you, it doesn't die. It just laughs and twirls its imaginary moustache.

Wasps are bastards and they know it. All they do all day is chew paper to make nests, hang around sticky drinks, and sting people for fun. And why is it that, on the one day of the year when the weather is remotely bearable, the sun comes out and with it come the wasps? Why don't the little gits ever go skiing or something? Then at least they might break their stupid wasp waists and we could all have a good laugh. But no, hot day, wasp. Sod off, wasps, and take flies with you. As humans, we prefer the company of daddy-long-legses.

CITY PIGEONS
∼

Let's differentiate here. There are some fine pigeons in the world. Real credits to society. Your wood pigeon is virtually a saint. It makes a nice noise, and it is pretty. Also in a pie it's OK. Racing pigeons are the greyhounds of the sky, noble beasts of the air who could find a pin in the Gobi Desert if, for some reason, they wanted to. But city pigeons are vile. Airborne sewers with guano so toxic it will burn through the paintwork of your car like bird's arse napalm.

Flying rats, you say? Hardly. People would pay money to see a flying rat. Aerodynamically graceful, sleek and with a wavy tail, a flying rat might be fun to see. A rat has character, it's a rat, not just a non-flying pigeon. Pigeons, on the other hand, are crap. Leaving aside the

... pigeons will come along and empty their bowels over everything and everyone

hereditary syphilis thing or whatever that is, they ought to be Cockney doves of the air, surviving on a diet of jellied eels and olive branches in the mean city streets. But they're not. They're brick-thick, filthy, one-toed nerks. They're not actually animals, they're machines designed for turning birdseed into guano. Good skill there, pigeon chappy.

And as for those old women who have nothing better to do than go out and spread the contents of their breadbins all over your local green space so that pigeons will come along and empty their bowels over everything and everyone – wouldn't you just love to see one of those old dears feeding the pigeons one sunny morning and suddenly an umarked van screech up, the doors fly open and four masked men leap out, throw her in the back and she's never seen again?

Better than a fine, any day of the week.

HOTELS

'It's the idea that thousands of potentially incontinent businessmen or absent-minded serial killers have stayed here before you.'

HOTEL ROOMS

~

Hotel rooms are like real rooms, only about nine times pokier and a hundred times more depressing. There's something deeply gloomy about staying in a hotel. Possibly it's the idea that thousands of potentially incontinent businessmen or absent-minded serial killers who just may have forgotten to take the severed head out of the safe when they left have stayed here before you. Possibly it's the ambience, that strange dim hotel room atmosphere which is part East German brothel in a spy movie and part overdressed cabin on a gay trawler. And possibly it's simply the knowledge that doing anything apart from opening the window will cost you a fortune; the minibar, the phone, the pay TV – if they could find a way to put a meter on the chocolate on the pillow they would.

HOTEL BATHROOMS

~

Awful places. For a start, they're often beige which is depressing. Instead of shampoo and soap and toothpaste, they have 'toiletries'. Toiletries are the smallest amounts of shampoo, soap and toothpaste that can actually be held. (Despite this, after you've used them, there's always some left which has to be either thrown away or drunk by the manager).

The shower curtain is made of some special clinging plastic which moulds itself to the shape of your cold wet body and allows the shower to spray the whole room with water. Which in turn forces you to mop it all up with the tiny towels they've provided for your face. (You can't use the big towels because of 'ecology'. See HOTEL TOWELS) And they think it's posh to have a phone in the bathroom. Handy, that, when you're in the shower. Who phones people from the shower? Norman Bates? 'Hi, I can't talk, I'm stabbing someone to death. Please leave a message after the scary violins.'

HOTEL TOWELS

Hotels already cost a fortune to stay in, but it's not enough for the 'hoteliers', as they call themselves only because they don't know the French for 'thieving bastards in cheap suits', to overcharge

you, they have to go one worse step further. Go into the bathroom and you will find a little sign, generally placed near the shower curtain. This sign will say something like this:

> HELP PROTECT THE ENVIRONMENT! TO PREVENT
> UNNECESSARY USE OF WATER AND ENVIRONMENTALLY
> DAMAGING DETERGENTS, WE ASK YOU TO REUSE
> YOUR TOWELS

There are two things you can do here. One is be a big old wimp and carefully dry yourself with little sections of the towel so as to prevent the Brazilian rainforests from tumbling into the mighty ocean. And the other is to dry yourself on every single scrap of cloth in the room, including the curtains and the shoe-polishing cloth, and then put this sign up next to their one.

> I AM THE ENVIRONMENT AND I AM SICK
> OF BEING BLAMED FOR THE FACT THAT YOU
> BASTARDS CAN'T BE BOTHERED TO WASH
> YOUR TOWELS EVERY DAY. I DON'T COME
> ROUND YOUR HOUSE AND TELL YOU TO REUSE
> YOUR FACE FLANNELS SO LEAVE ME ALONE.
> P.S. I HAVE STOLEN THE DRESSING GOWN AND
> THE WEIRD FLAT SLIPPERS.

That should do the trick.

HOTEL TV

Leaving aside the thorny issue of pay TV – you've already paid the hotel enough money to buy your own television set, and now they want to charge you so you can watch *Star Wars IX: Mission To Moscow* or some other old rubbish you wouldn't even get out on DVD if Hollywood burned to the ground tomorrow – what the hell are they doing giving themselves their own channel? And 'TV' itself is a pretty loose description of something that's in fact nothing more than a photograph of a simpleton in a bellboy's uniform with the words

*Welcome to the
Grandisson Edwarditorian*

written over his face in the kind of typeface that is normally reserved for wedding invitations. They could be using the channel to show something useful, like where the local pubs are or how to fiddle the mini-bar.

HOTEL KEYS
❧

The word here is 'key'. Metal thing, round at one end, squiggly at the other. Goes in a keyhole, you turn it and the door opens. Easy. That's a key. What's not a key is this; a piece of plastic the size and shape of a credit card with some little holes in it that you put in a slot in a door and hope the green light goes 'beep' and you don't have to go all the way back down to reception for another piece of plastic that doesn't work either.

MUZAK
❧

The sound, not of hell, because that would be at least exciting, but of grey. Muzak is what zombies listen to in their dead cars. It's a depressing trickle of onanising strings from a cheap speaker mounted somewhere above your head like a security camera that, instead of recording crime, emits it.

TIPPING
❧

Tipping is one of the greatest evils known to man. The case for it is a simple one; people in menial jobs do not earn enough money. This is true. There can be nothing worse than going round cleaning up after people, dragging heavy objects around and so forth for minimum wages. Only a fool or a sadist would say that this is a good thing. However, this is not your fault. You are not personally responsible for paying people low wages. We didn't have the Tolpuddle Martyrs and 300 years of trade union activism just so you could end up helping staff make up their awful wages. When you are at your own place of work, the boss doesn't come up to you and say, 'I'm afraid I can't be bothered to pay you a decent wage this month – tell you what, there's a couple of American tourists outside, they might bung you a fiver'.

THE ROADS

'A 30 mph limit in a village is a sensible thing. A 30 mph limit on a dual carriageway where some workmen went home two days ago is not.'

SPEED BUMPS

A lso known as 'sleeping policemen', either because speed bumps enable real traffic cops to spend more time in bed, or to make less bright drivers slow down because they think an actual policeman is asleep in the middle of the road. The whole language of speed bumps, in fact, is pretty odd. Take the phrase 'traffic calming'. It's

unclear how traffic is supposed to be 'calmed' by being slowed down to four mph while cars have the bejesus whacked out of their chassis and the old chap in front of you is approaching each bump as though it were the River Styx itself. But speed bumps are designed to calm traffic, if not nerves, and they do work. In the sense that pouring thousands of gallons of glue into the road would work.

There's the cost – the cheapest speed bump costs £2000 in London. (The cost of the most expensive speed bump built is unknown, but it was believed to

have been one that was specially commissioned as an engagement present from Ben Affleck to Jennifer Lopez, and shaped exactly like her bottom).

Speed bumps are actually dangerous. Houses are burning down because fire engines get held up by the old chap in front of them while critically ill patients are having seizures in ambulances as they bounce over the bumps like cumbersome white jet-skis. This is true. According to the London Ambulance Service, up to 500 deaths a year are attributable to humps, because of the delays they cause to ambulances. Meanwhile in Yorkshire 40 new ambulances had to be taken off the road because they grounded on speed bumps. Oh, and there's the pollution thing. A study by the Transport Research Laboratory claimed that on roads with humps, emissions from cars of carbon monoxide increased by between 30% and 60%, carbon dioxide rose between 20% and 26%, while nitrous oxide and emissions from diesel-powered vehicles were up to 30% higher.

Apart from that, they're great.

SPEED CAMERAS

Guaranteed to sometimes stop people speeding on any stretch of road where there is one. And then make up the lost time by hurtling like maniacs down the next cameraless stretch of road. Also, often located in bits of road where the speed limit sign is clearly having a laugh. A 30 mph limit in a village is a sensible thing. A 30 mph limit on a dual carriageway where some workmen went home two days ago is not.

PARKING METERS

They don't work. People with lots of spare time and coins have proved it, by putting money in and timing meters. You frequently don't get the full hour. But just try to get a refund and you'll spend billions on stamps, ink and whatever you drink when you get annoyed.

And that's not even mentioning out-of-service meters. There is nothing sadder, and more suspicious, than an out-of-service parking

meter. With a bag over its head and a hangdog air, out-of-service parking meters look like hostages. They're not; you are – a hostage to random parking decisions. Why are these meters out of service? Were they wounded in some bizarre traffic warden shoot out? Have they nobly sacrificed themselves – 'You go on without me, sarge, I'm just a burden to the other meters'? Or are they just publicity-shy? Perhaps there is a *Heat* magazine for parking meters, and the ones with bags over their heads are the equivalent of those celebrities you see wearing their unconvincing disguise of baseball cap, sunglasses and hooded sweat-top. Oh, apparently it's something to do with roadworks or sewage or the phones. Here's an idea; maybe everyone who digs up the roads could get together and organise their jobs so they're not digging up your parking spot 365 days a year.

CLAMPING

⌒

The wheel clamp was originally known as 'the Denver Boot' until they realised that no-one knew or cared what that meant. Now it is know simply as 'the wheel clamp' or something ruder. Wheel clamps are a triumph of technology over ideas. Just as cloning and genetic experiments have led to questionable moral decisions that nobody has thought through, so clamping is an invention that seemed to make life easier, but in fact has done nothing but wreak havoc.

The reason for inventing the clamp was simple: to keep the streets clear of traffic by penalising drivers and making them put their cars somewhere else. The effect of using the clamp is slightly different. It stops cars moving, thereby paralysing traffic as effectively as if someone had gone round chloroforming every driver on the

> . . . clamping is an invention that seemed to make life easier, but in fact has wrought nothing but havoc.

road. Not only that, those notices they put on the windscreen are really embarrassing. They might as well save ink and just print HA HA in big red letters on them. Oh, and not only do you have to pay for the clamp, the parking ticket is on top of that. Lovely

N.B. Clamping is a double-edged sword. On the one hand, there is nothing worse than finding a stupid iron triangle attached to your rear wheel like it was in love with your car. On the other hand, there is no more joyful sight than seeing someone else's car being hoisted up onto a flatbed truck to be taken away and, quite possibly, thrown into a quarry.

MINICABS

Not to be confused with black cabs (see BLACK CABS), minicabs are taxis in the way that two bits of old sacks tied together in the middle with string are clothing. The criteria for being a minicab do not vary from nation to nation or continent to continent. To be a minicab, a car must fulfil the following criteria:

- *It must have the world's oldest magic tree air freshener hanging from the rear-view mirror.*

- *The rear-view mirror is the only mirror the car possesses. It is there solely to support the magic tree.*

- *One of the doors is a different colour to all of the other doors. It may even be from a different type of car entirely. In special cases, the door may not be from a car, but from a henhouse, or a cellar.*

- *The car radio only plays radio stations that you did not know you could get in Abergavenny or Redcar, like Radio Completely Mad Turkish Bloke or Religious Maniac FM. It crackles and hisses and goes WEEEE OOOOO WEEE because it is never quite tuned in properly, even if the car is parked directly underneath the massive intercontinental aerial serving Religious Maniac FM.*

- *There is a cassette player. Somehow, this too crackles and hisses and goes WEEEE OOOOO WEEE.*

There are many and various kinds of minicab driver, because the reasons that force men to become minicab drivers are themselves many and various. Some men become minicab drivers because they enjoy their own company, some because divorce and redundancy has left them no other option. Most minicab drivers, however, become minicab drivers because they are bastard mental and love nothing more than driving round cities they do not know very well at appalling speeds. They are like some strange form of disgraced test pilot, condemned to spend their lives testing the worst and oldest cars in the world.

And where black cab drivers study for years to gain the Knowledge, minicab drivers seem to undergo some kind of reverse procedure, possibly called the Ignorance. No minicab driver has even the slightest concept of geography. World landmarks such as Buckingham Palace, Times Square and the Champs-Elysées are as mysterious to them as the moons of Jupiter. New York minicab drivers are unable to tell you the name of the street between Second Avenue and Fourth Avenue. Berlin minicab drivers do not know that the Wall has come down, and drive around town looking for it like it owes them money. If they had had minicabs in the Roman empire, they would somehow have managed to find at least one road that did not lead to Rome.

If they had had minicabs in the Roman empire, they would somehow have managed to find at least one road that did not lead to Rome.

Minicab drivers make up for this complete lack of geography by driving as fast as possible. In the same way as tourists who don't speak the language try to compensate by shouting instead, minicab drivers seem to think that if you drive really fast, this will stop you getting lost. It doesn't; it just means that after 25 minutes you run out of petrol on a really rough housing estate 15 miles outside town and the moment you get out of the car to help the driver look for the petrol can, lots of people with dead eyes and their arms sticking out straight in front of them appear from nowhere.

There is one further, more disturbing thing about minicab drivers. Payment. Most of us, if we have a job which involves taking money off people and possibly giving them change, might lay on a small supply of coins and low denomination notes. Your average minicab driver, however, is always taken utterly by surprise when someone tells him they don't have the exact fare, which strongly suggests that he has no other money with him, a fact which itself suggests that you are the only fare he has had this evening, or possibly today, or more likely ever.

BLACK CABS

1) THE KNOWLEDGE. This is supposed to give London cab drivers the ability to find any street in London. In reality, it gives them the ability to know that where you live is just far enough out of their way for them to refuse to take you.

2) THE RIVER THAMES. It's a river. It has bridges over it. It is populated on each side, both sides being equally Londonish. It is not a nuclear wasteland or a dense impenetrable forest where black cabs cannot penetrate. 'Sorry, mate, I don't go south of the river,' really means 'Sorry, mate, I'm a bone idle Cockney git too exhausted from talking bollocks all day to drive over a bridge.'

3) 'I KNEW THE KRAYS'. No, you didn't. You weren't a runner for them, they never gave you a shilling and ruffled your hair, your older sister didn't go out with one of their drivers and they didn't buy every kid in your street a toy fire-engine. The nearest you got to the Krays was seeing that film with the men from Spandau Ballet in.

4) GOODNESS ME, HAS LONDON REALLY CHANGED SUCH A LOT IN THE 50 YEARS THAT HAVE PASSED SINCE YOU WERE A BOY? Well I never. Knock me down with a feather. The rest of the country is

gripped in a terrible stasis the like of which has not been seen since the Black Death.

5) TALKING BOLLOCKS (part one). For people in a profession who, by definition, meet literally hundreds of people every week, from all walks of life, creeds, colours and beliefs, cab drivers really do seem to know bugger all about anything. They still believe that foreign people take all our jobs, that the country is being ruined by the unions and (in one genuine, rather scary instance endured by the author) that the music industry pays *Top of the Pops* to feature black music instead of 'proper music like Cliff Richard'.

6) TRAVEL. How is it that, despite taking an impressive range of foreign holidays, cab drivers know nothing about their own country. A cabbie can bang on for days about Alicante and Majorca, Florida and Tunisia, but mention Lancashire or Wales or the Isle of Wight and you'll be lucky if they say, 'I did me national service there.'

N.B. There are two exceptions to this rule. All cabbies know the West Country because they have a caravan there. And they all know the Isle of Man because they still have, or used to have, corporal punishment. 'That would sort 'em out.' 'Sort out who?' 'Yeah. Anyway.'

> All cabbies know the West Country because they have a caravan there.

7) TALKING BOLLOCKS (part two). All cab drivers take it as a given that the real reason you got in their taxi is not to get home, but for a nice chat (or, more specifically, for a nice listen). Nothing can stop a chatty cabbie from going off on an epic monologue. You can shut the little glass window, and he'll turn on the intercom. You can nod and grunt and he'll take this as signs of extreme pleasure. Oh, and never ever make the mistake of getting out a book or a paper or rummaging about for your Walkman. To a cab driver, these are the emblems of the lonely, symbols of a person who is desperate for human company. Be warned.

TRENDY SCOOTERS
〜

Scooter, *noun.* A not very good attempt at doing a motorbike for people who are scared to go more than 20 mph but are embarrassed to actually own a moped or a bicycle or a penny-farthing, possibly (see PENNY-FARTHING).

Trendy scooter, *noun.* As above, only supposed to be fashionable and mod, in the way that owning a snail and painting an RAF roundel on its shell is fashionable and mod. Generally owned by celebrity chefs, pretend rock stars, members of the media and people who saw Quadrophenia once too often (i.e. four times).

URBAN CYCLISTS
〜

Are they a car? They act like one half the time – taking up a whole lane so you have to drive along looking at their smug bony backsides, parking right in front of you at traffic lights so you either have to let them go first or ram right up their aforementioned smug bony backsides. Oh, but then they decide they aren't a car, and ride through a red light, or cycle along the pavement, whacking pedestrians, because they're too sodding idle to use a one-way system.

City cyclists have a unique combination of smugness and laziness that previously was only found in members of the French aristocracy and law students. They have all their crappy paraphernalia that, they think, marks them out as exciting gypsies of the cycle route –

Oh, but then they decide they aren't a car, and ride through a red light, or cycle along the pavement, whacking pedestrians, because they're too sodding idle to use a one-way system.

their stupid helmets, their masks, their Lycra body-stocking, which is meant to show us how superfast they are, but in reality just shows us how small their genitals are. They go on cycling 'protests', which are meant to demonstrate the evils of the internal combustion engine, but only reveal what we all knew, that urban cyclists are arrogant dicks who think they have the right to plough through town, ringing their noncing bells, cutting old ladies up at corners and generally behaving like the kind of worthless pedal pillocks who in a perfect world would be given a special cycle lane that led into a deep, cold, water-logged mine-shaft. With sharks in.

MOUNTAIN BIKES

After the bizarre aberration of the penny-farthing (see PENNY-FARTHING), bicycles settled down to being, well, just bikes. There was a time when a bike was a pushbike. This was a good name for them. They were pushbikes and most of the time you pushed them. Bikes were unthreatening, unexciting and about as sexy as being married to some porridge. And then some fool invented the mountain bike. This was as much like the pushbike as a toy glider from a newsagent is like the ME109, that is to say, not absurdly different, but different enough to make some git who likes tight-fitting clothes and wearing a helmet get too excited.

Mountain bikes are fast. They are dramatic. They either weigh a ton and thus are very manly, or they are made off some metal that Doctor Who invented and weigh less than a stamp and are thus very futuristic. They are designed to be rugged, which is useful in town or country, and covetable by thieves, which is not. This causes their owners to dress them down, and paint them drab colours, which makes them non-covetable, so that only their owners love them. What is the point of that? You don't get rich ladies giving their diamond necklaces a respray with some khaki paint or wrapping a bit of gaffer tape around their wedding rings, but that's what happens with posh bikes. You might as well get a pushbike.

PENNY-FARTHING
◡

What in the name of all the burning souls of the damned in hell below were they thinking?

'Good morning, Professor Nemo. Have you invented anything for me today?'

'Good day to you, Prince Rupert of Nancystein. Yes, I have. It is a new improved form of velocipede.'

'Oh. I was rather hoping it wasn't a velocipede this time. I've already got nine.'

'But this is a different kind of velocipede, your richesty. It has a completely different motive alignment.'

'Oh wow. What does that mean?'

'The front wheel is bigger than the back wheel.'

'What?'

'The front wheel is bigger than the back wheel. Loads bigger.'

'How much bigger?'

'Really quite a lot. I mean, the back one, you can hardly see it. You could barely use it as a steering wheel on a Smart car.'

'What's a Smart car?'

'Never mind. And the front wheel – it's bloody ridiculous. It's twice the size of a cartwheel. You need a stepladder just to change the tyre.'

'Well, it's different, I suppose. Does it have an exciting method of propulsion?'

'Yes. The pedals are in the middle of the big wheel.'

'Why doesn't it have a chain?'

'A chain? Are you mad? If that comes off and you haven't got your stepladder with you, you'll never get it back on again.'

'Oh sod it, I'll take six. Five solid gold ones and one made of, I don't know, lark's tongues. That'll show the Kaiser.'

FOOD

'Like a beautiful woman who knows you'll do anything she says because you want some sex, a bad restaurant knows you will put up with any old appallingness because you're hungry. '

BURGER BARS

～

How is a burger bar a bar? Bars are, if memory serves correctly, places where the conversation and the wine flow, the atmosphere is convivial, and people gather to meet and enjoy each other's company. Bars are not greasy old crapholes full of unhappy exam failures on a minimum wage who are forced to stand behind a counter listening to the so-called food requests of people who don't know what fruit and vegetables are.

Bits of old tyres and plastic remodelled to resemble food.

From the fantastically British hell of the Wimpy burger bar – which is in fact a greasy spoon that saw a picture of America once – to the slick corporate grin of Burger King, burger bars are all the same. Bits of old tyres and plastic remodelled to resemble food. Because, no matter how much McDonald's go on obsessively and neurotically about how their burgers are 10,000% beef and their salads are handplucked from the Garden of Eden, they cannot disguise the essential truth; they sell greasy old rubbish which is good for you in the same way that six hours watching donkey porn is good for you i.e. you might enjoy it in a weird way but somewhere out there you dimly suspect there might be a better, more wholesome life.

Is it coincidence that McDonald's company symbol is a clown? (see CLOWNS) No, of course it isn't. Because like clowns, McDonald's 'restaurants' are horrible frightening things posing as sources of fun and laughter. If Ronald McDonald was a real person – well, if Ronald McDonald was a real person, he'd have been beaten to death by now, but apart from that, if he was real, he wouldn't be larking about with Mayor Chuffburglar and Hamface or whatever his stupid fake toy tie-in mates are called. He'd be wearing a shellsuit and standing hunched in a queue with three kids with chocolate and snot all over their faces wondering if a Happy Meal would ever make him really happy, and if Mrs McDonald wants a too-hot apple pie. When in fact Mrs McDonald is back at home, at it like knives with Colonel Sanders. Probably.

CELEBRITY CHEFS
∾

O h great, you can cook. And you can read an autocue. Clearly you are deserving of vast wealth and fame. Mechanics are more useful than chefs, in that we can all heat food up and eat it, but we can't all fix our own cars. Nurses even more so. But we don't have celebrity mechanics or famous nurses.

The fact that a proper chef writes all your recipes because you are in reality only trained to make chips need not deter your upward path. You are a celebrity chef. You will appear in adverts for food that have exactly the opposite effect to the one desired, i.e. they make right-thinking people want to throw up. You 'write' books that have no more than five recipes in them and a photograph of an aubergine. And for some reason you go to non-food-related movie premieres.

You 'write' books that have no more than five recipes in them and a photograph of an aubergine

The only celebrity chef TV show we need is one where chefs compete to feed a ravenous man-eating tiger, and if the tiger doesn't like their cooking, he gets to eat them. Now that would be compulsive viewing.

TAKE-AWAY PIZZA PARLOURS
∾

F irst off, what's this 'parlour' business? It gives the impression that pizzas are made in the front rooms of elderly Victorian spinsters, who are taking a few minutes off starching their antimacassars and putting gussets on the piano legs.

There is something extraordinarily weird about pizza parlours or expresses or lands or huts (and what's that all about? You expect to find workman's lanterns or medieval peasants in a hut, not pizzas, surely). They are invariably staffed by a lone grim-faced nine-year-old

harridan who will be ready to take your order as soon as she has fin-
ished flirting in a blood-curling manner with the chef. After taking
four days to write down your order, she will then get it completely
wrong. Now this is not necessarily an incomprehensible thing. After
all, consider the average menu of the average pizza place. There are a
lot of things on that menu, true. Different toppings and kinds of
bread and drinks and choices. It's a cornucopia of heated bread with
tomato sauce on top of its delights. Understandably, sometimes
someone will get the order slightly wrong if it is rather complicated.
We all make mistakes.

What's harder to understand is that, by some twisted distortion of
the laws of logic, the people who take your order in pizza parlours
will generally get the harder orders right, and the easy ones completely wrong. Thin crust extra-large sloppy prawn quatro formaggio
with extra mushroom and no tomato? Piece of cake. Large pepperoni
and bottle of cola? You jest, sirrah. You might get spicy chicken
wings, a quart of Lilt and the crown jewels of Lithuania, but you
won't get what you ordered.

No-one knows why this is.

HOT-DOG VENDORS

〜

Anyone seen *Oliver!*? Remember that delightful song where all the
Victorian street traders are hawking their wares and Oliver
introduces the notion of selling a beautiful morning, on the grounds
that such a sky he never did see, which seems a bit cruel to the beautiful morning, especially given that six scenes ago Oliver himself had
been sold, by Harry Secombe. Anyway, the good thing about that
scene is how all the Victorian street traders have their own little songs
about whatever they're selling, flowers and strawberries and even the
knife-grinder has a little knife-grinding song.

These days, of course, street vendors are reduced to students in
tabards (see CHARITY STUDENTS IN TABARDS), the odd chestnut seller,
some dubious Cockney with a milk-crate covered in fake perfume,
and, that stalwart of late night urban life, the hot-dog vendor.

There are two things about hot-dog vendors worth mentioning straight up. One, no way are those things hot dogs. They are kind of loaves with pig lips embedded in them. And two, these people are, in essence, mobile kebab shops. They may not be selling actual kebabs, but then nor are the people who run kebab shops. They are selling fake nutrition to people who aren't actually hungry, but are what doctors call 'beer hungry', i.e. they are so pissed that they think they are hungry. Were it legal and economical for late night street vendors to sell wigs dipped in brown sauce, they'd do that. And drunk people would eat 'em.

BAD RESTAURANTS

Bastards. Like a beautiful woman who knows you'll do anything she says because you want some sex, a bad restaurant knows you will put up with any old appallingness because you're hungry. And the appallingness you have to put up with would fill any menu they might come up with.

For starters (hey!), even getting past the door is a pain in the face. You can't sit down in even the emptiest restaurants without being vetted. You walk in and immediately you get halted by some fake French fool in a cheap tuxedo. 'Two?' he asks, in case you were thinking of sneaking 75 other people in later on. 'Do you have a reservation?' he will then add, even though the restaurant is completely empty and will remain so until it goes bust and becomes a Starbucks in three months' time. You confirm that you do have a reservation and he looks like he might cry. Now he has to actually do some work.

He shows you to the worst table in the room. Again, even though the place is empty, you won't be given a decent place to eat. This is on the off-chance Terry Wogan or Superman comes in and wants your

> You walk in and immediately
> you get halted by some fake French fool
> in a cheap tuxedo.

table. If you object to your table, on the grounds that it is actually in the toilet, he will look sullen and put you behind a pillar.

By now, several minutes have elapsed since you came in. Your stomach is churning and growling like a Rottweiler made of acid. You want a drink the way Tom Waits wants a drink. And you are still no nearer to having any food.

You sit down. And now the waiter vanishes. This is so you can ponder the folly of your ways. After a bit, or when you notice the waiter putting his coat on, you decide to summon him. He is strangely blind to your hand signals, but does eventually notice you when you run across the room and knock him to the ground.

'We'd like to see a menu, please,' you say, and again he looks pained, as though most of his customers memorised the menu before they came out. Some time later, you will get a menu. The waiter tells you that there are some specials on the blackboard. This blackboard has been placed somewhere visually challenging, like behind a pillar, or down a corridor, or possibly in a secret chamber.

You and your companion have chosen what you want to eat. You have consulted the wine list and done that thing where you pick the third cheapest wine so as not to appear a total skinflint. Now your stomach is actually consuming itself, you're so hungry. The waiter finishes listening to some enormous Belgian telling him the story of his life and accidentally walks back past your table. You grab his greasy sleeve and make him take your order.

Time passes. The breadsticks are demolished. The wine is drunk long before the food arrives. Then the food arrives. It is someone else's food. The right food arrives. It is cold. This is because it was prepared some time ago but nobody made the connection between it and the people in the big room with all the tables.

This process is repeated all through the various courses. Then the most puzzling thing of all happens. It is time to pay. Now, it makes some stupid sense for restaurant staff to disappear when you want to order food or see a menu or demand help with the Heimlich manoeuvre. They're not getting anything out of it. But paying the bill is different. You want to give them money, so you can go. You may even have a tip for them. But they have vanished.

'Table nine want the bill.'

'Quick! Let's all hide in the meat freezer!'

Eventually a waiter will come out and give you the bill. He will then disappear again for up to 70 minutes. This is to give you time to play Spot The 15 Deliberate Mistakes with the bill. Fortunately, not only do you have an excellent memory, you've also brought a calculator. After a lot of work, you produce a version of the bill that bears some relation to reality, and offer to pay that. The waiter, realising the jig is up, accepts your credit card. But what's this he sees? Snootily, he jabs a finger at the bill. 'It says service NOT included,' he says.

This is where you say, 'Yes, and we didn't get any service,' and run like hell.

SUPERMARKETS

Giant stadiums of consumer hell, designed to depress us and remove all character and individuality from the shattered ruins of our souls. And that's on a good day. Given that torching the sods is illegal and you may burn your fingers while doing so, here are a few pointers for supermarket owners.

1) To save the nation's youth from themselves, why not put all the sweets and chewing gum up the back where the spotty little buggers might have to make some effort to get them? And put the fruit and veg next to the tills instead so maybe the nation's future might pick up something nutritious on the way out.

2) How about making 'reward' cards actually rewarding? Currently they resemble rewards not much at all.

REWARD!
FOR SPENDING ALL YOUR MONEY IN OUR STORE
AND NOT AN IDENTICAL RIVAL NEARBY!
**ONE WHOLE PENNY BACK PER EVERY
HUNDRED POUNDS SPENT!***

*Unless we change our minds or get bought by our identical rivals,
in which case all points are void.

---

3) And stop that thing where whenever you go in, they've always run out of whatever meat or fish or veg or fruit you want, except oddly in the organic section, where there's tons, so you buy it, even though it's twice as dear and tastes slightly of wee.

4) What's with this mass corporate greed thing? Granted, it's nice not to have to go to an over-priced local shop where the staff get paid in groats and a jar of marmalade costs £15, but there are limits.

5) And you're buggering up other areas. Stick to food. Selling cheap books and CDs is great if you're a Danielle Steele or Westlife fan, but anybody who has a slighter wider range of interests is stuffed. And just as bad money drives out good, so rubbish R'n'B and pretend Bridget Jones books will drive out everything else.

SUPERMARKET TROLLEYS

❧

Wire-faced crap wagons. Who designed them? A village idiot in the last stages of DTs? The cart must have been one of the first things invented by primitive man, and since medieval times, we've been getting quite good at building simple four-wheeled vehicles. Some of them even have engines now.

But supermarket trolleys are an evolutionary throwback to the time of the Flintstones. They've got four wheels. They steer forwards and sideways. They're not meant to crash into the beans display every fourteen seconds while simultaneously crushing your toes and wrenching your arm out of its socket as you try to make the bastard go right instead of into your groin.

Just a tiny fault on a single wheel causes the useless chariot of pain to blunder up and down the aisles like a gored robot or develop an alarming hobble as it bangs up and down like a trapdoor in a gale. It would be safer and more efficient if supermarket staff gave us sleds pulled by alcoholic huskies to trawl our goods around with.

THE FRENCH

'No other country to have created its own blueprint for the toilet has ever come up with anything so spectacularly useless.'

PARISIANS

~

French people are famous amongst the English for being haughty and unfriendly, refusing to speak any language other than their own and being rude a lot. Put this to a French person and they will say, 'Not me, mate, you're thinking of the Parisians.' Because when it comes to sheer naked bloody-minded arrogance, there is one city in the whole wide world which takes the sheer naked bloody-minded arrogant biscuit every time, La Belle Bastarde Paris.

For some reason the good people of Paris think they are it just because every morning they wake up and see a poor copy of the Blackpool Tower looking down on them. As a city, their main achievements are inventing the Cancan, giving Napoleon somewhere to live, storming the Bastille and living on cats during the Franco-Prussian War. Not much to boast about there. Yet to see them snickering away because you can't say 'baguette' properly, you'd think they had invented space travel. Not devoted their stupid lives to pretending that Jerry Lewis is funny.

FRENCH MUSIC

~

What's that racket? Has a cat got into the air-conditioning? It seems to be coming from outside that quaint French pavement cafe. Oh, it's some French musicians.

French music, as a genre, is doomed from the start, as every French song has to feature the accordion, and you're not going to get very far with that as a basis for your national *musique*. Accordions only exist because sailors found they couldn't strap pianos to their chests, so they invented a sort of horrible wheezing portable piano. And for some reason, perhaps because they had been at the absinthe, the French found the melancholy tones of the accordion strangely alluring.

They also invented another equally unnecessary musical form; the jazz guitar, Now, jazz sounds at its best when played by raging trumpets and barking saxophones. It sounds completely useless when played on the acoustic guitar, whose capacity for expressiveness is somewhat limited by the fact that it consists of six plastic strings draped over a wooden hole and consequently when Monsieur Jazz goes off on one, all he can do is make plinky plinky noises.

The French are also rubbish at rock music.

The French are also rubbish at rock music. French rock'n'roller Johnny Halliday has never crossed over in this country, despite being quite a bit more rocking than our own Cliff Richard. Perhaps this is because what the French like best about rock is the attitude – all that rather dated leather jacket, cigarette and motorbike stuff. To the French, that says, 'Vive le rock.' To the rest of the world, it says, 'I like men.'

FRENCH HOTELS
～

While it's unfair to single out the hotel accommodations of one nation over any other – and certainly every country can boast its share of bad hotels – there ought to be special mention made of French hotels. Not the delightful auberges and pensions that dot the countryside with their bucolic delights and amusing local vintages, but the big buggers in the towns and cities. For some reason (see FRENCH DESIGN), the French have very special ideas as to what constitutes a proper hotel.

There are certain regular items that you will find in any French hotel, which suggests that they are doing it deliberately. The star rating is always one, and arguably two, higher than it ought to be, so that hotels which in the rest of Europe would be found next to a railway station or a murderer's park have the kind of rating that the Dorchester might struggle to achieve, while the actual one-star hotels resemble the headquarters of one of Captain Kirk's more primitive enemies. The plumbing is always of an *Antiques Roadshow* standard, and the pipes really do make that DONGDONGDONGDONGDONG DONG noise that they normally only do in old sitcoms.

The bed is as small as a bed can be without actually being a matchbox with sheets on it. The carpet is an enlarged rug apparently won from a heavy smoker in a game of whist. And, weirdest of all, there is the television. This is invariably the smallest TV you have ever seen, and its tininess is accentuated by the fact that, to prevent it being accidentally swallowed by a child, it has been attached to the ceiling on a bracket. There is a remote control, but the batteries have been taken out, and the TV can only be operated by climbing onto the radiator and hitting it. When the set does come on, however, it only gets the news in Algerian and the most frightening blue movie you have ever seen.

This is invariably the smallest TV you have ever seen, and its tininess is accentuated by the fact that, to prevent it being accidentally swallowed by a child, it has been attached to the ceiling on a bracket.

FRENCH DESIGN
❧

There is a danger of this book being confused with something anti-French. But this is not a right assumption. The French are one of the great peoples of the world. Their beautiful language, their contributions to art, music, literature and of course food and drink are immeasurable. Even the legendary rudeness of Parisians is still preferable to the ravings of London cab drivers. But they are, for a nation living, in fact, a short walk away from us, very different from the British. And this is best seen in their design.

The rest of the world has a very sensible attitude to design. Someone invents something – a car, an airplane, a legal system – and after a while everyone else either nicks the idea or comes up with a superior variant. This is why most cars, say, are streamlined, shiny and

comfortable. This is why military vehicles, for example, look hard and tough and a bit sexy. And this is why lemon squeezers look really boring. But the French do not give a toss about any of this. Their cars look like they have been folded up out of bits of cardboard, like origami cars. Their tanks seem to be made of Lego. And their lemon squeezers – well, your great-granny would turn in her grave.

FRENCH TOILETS
∽

French design taken to its ultimate. No other country to have created its own blueprint for the toilet has ever come up with anything so spectacularly useless. They might as well hang a big sign on the border that says, 'WE HAVE NO CONCEPT OF HYGIENE.' From the revolting hole in the middle to the footrests – how thoughtful, that should stop people falling backwards into the revolting hole – the entire facility is designed to make your life really, really unpleasant. No wonder it is rumoured that many French people prefer to take their chances *dans la rue*.

Their cars look like they have been folded up out of bits of cardboard, like origami cars.

LEISURE

*'Abroad has beaches and resorts and lagoons
and marinas. Britain has 'seaside'.*

CARAVANS

Caravans take their name from a shimmering procession of Arabian merchants wending their way across the desert, head-dresses a-flutter in the breeze, noble camels bearing spices of the orient. If Lawrence of Arabia saw a British caravan clanking up the A38 being towed by a guffing Datsun Cherry, he'd turn in his grave. A few thoughts for the clanky highwaymen:

1. Good-looking chaps, ain't they? No. They look like the incestuous children of Portakabins and mobile burger bars. They clog up the roads, they blight the landscape, and the only good thing about being in them is you're the only person who can't actually see 'em.

2. What's with the names? Caravans potter up the motorway at 14 mph, clanking along with neither grace nor speed. They spend half their lives sitting in fields like a broken donkey. In fact, a good name for a caravan would be 'Eeyore' or 'Mister Lump'. But they're not called that. Caravans are always given names like 'Challenger', 'Motivator' or 'Dragonwing'. Giving caravans exciting, dynamic names must make the owners feel they are towing some sort of Cruise missile up the M3.

3. Who would live in a place like this? Well, comfortably, no-one, except some midgets. The reason you always see people in caravans sitting on a banquette playing ludo on a folding Formica table is not because that's what they want to do, it's because they're stuck. They've been there for three days. They hate ludo. They're surviving by eating the cards from the Happy Families pack. Caravans are cramped like overcrowded horizontal lifts. No room to sit, eat, talk, watch the static-fizzing telly or sleep.

4. The chemical toilet. Oh what a joy.

5. Caravan sites. There is a reason hotels were invented. It is so that no-one would ever have to get out of their tiny bunk at six am, wash in an inch of soapy water next to a miniature vat of chemical horror (see 4) and then stagger across a field of dew-sodden grass to get a pint of milk and a *Daily Mail* from a one-eyed local lad in the most Eastern-European-looking Spar in the world.

THE BRITISH SEASIDE

'Oh, I do like to be beside the seaside,' says the old song. It then goes on to explain why, in a flurry of nonsense about brass bands playing tiddly om pom pom and stuff. Lyrically, it's a short song and it's not hard to see why. A song that went 'Oh, I don't like to be beside the seaside' would be a lot longer.

Abroad has beaches and resorts and lagoons and marinas. Britain has 'seaside'. A significant choice of word, that. 'Seaside' is not a word redolent of lounging by beautiful water on lush golden sands. It is a word redolent of 'sea' and 'side'. 'Seaside' is probably the only expression for British coastal leisure zones that wouldn't get in trouble

'Seaside' is probably the only expression for British coastal leisure zones that wouldn't get in trouble under the Trade Descriptions Act.

under the Trade Descriptions Act. Whatever anyone says about the seaside, there's no denying it's beside the sea.

After that, things get thornier. Our beaches are the pride of nowhere, unless hell has pride. More suitable for heaving landing craft up onto, or covering in barbed wire, British beaches have always been bleak, determined things, not so much a silken strand as the place where the land gave up. But what are the alternatives? Scare the wits out of the kids by taking them to a Punch and Judy show? Not likely; you might as well get *Driller Killer* out on DVD. Take them onto the pier? Sure, if you want them to meet the entire population of Essex on a thrill-seeking mission to spend as many two-pence pieces as possible.

Best stay on the beach. Of course, you'll need a windbreak, Britain being the only place in the world where you don't just need sun protection on the beach, you need protection from a howling force ten gale. And you'll need a tenner to hire deckchairs, Britain also being the kind of country where we love to charge people for the honour of sitting on some wet, sandy cloth attached to a rickety wooden frame. And you'll need something for the kids to do, because all the interesting animalcules that used to live in the rock pools are dead, and they're too scared to go in the water because the tide is out so far that you need a passport to go swimming because you have to wade out as far as Normandy to actually get enough water to doggy-paddle in.

Alternatively, you can do what most British holidaymakers love best. Sit in the car on the seafront in a hailstorm, eating fish paste sandwiches and looking out of the window.

AIRPORTS
∿

Airports are places that we are forced to spend many hours in. And, if you don't count shops and pubs and restaurants, there is nothing to do. Nothing whatsoever. So, if your flight is delayed a few hours or, let's be honest here, days, and you've exhausted the thrill of seeing how many different things can be made with a Burberry design, and how just totally exactly the same all the Burger Kings are

(Do the staff have a special meeting every day where they all agree on equal levels of greasiness?) then your alternatives for entertainment are:

• watching the weird TV set that only shows Saturday morning kids' TV, no matter what day of the week or time of night it is.

• enjoying the 'mini-arcade' which is three old Space Invaders machines (see 'CLASSIC') and a coin-operated Bob The Builder dumptruck that doesn't work.

None of these are in the least appealing to anyone over six years old. Seaside holiday boarding houses have got more entertainment facilities than airports. At Heathrow, there isn't even a drawer full of incomplete board games. Gatwick, for one, would be immensely improved by someone from Virgin Airlines (see VIRGIN) coming round and saying, 'Who wants a game of Risk with some of the pieces missing?'

AIRPORT BOOK STORES
∾

At home you might care to read a variety of literature. In an airport, it seems, you have turned into a drooling gibbon of near-illiteracy, if the choices are anything to go by. Thrillers, horror novels, science-fiction novels, pretend pornographic novels, actual pornographic novels with a black-and-white photo of someone with no head, books about women who want to get married that have a stupid drawing of a champagne glass or a high-heeled shoe on the front to indicate that they are 'fun', children's books that look like they might be a bit like Harry Potter but aren't... and, just to make the whole thing stupider, all of these books are available in special 'airport editions', which are the size of a small table. Just the thing to turn your carry-on baggage into something that goes in the hold. Not only that, but these giant editions remind the reader of the large print novels that their elderly aunt used to read with the aid of her enormospecs and thus brings the chill of age to mind.

LUGGAGEY SHOPS

A real danger. Walking round the airport, giant book in one hand, disgusting snack in the other, there is little to do but go into shops and look at things. You are unlikely to buy a tin of toffees from a little booth that thinks it's Harrods. Nor are you going to lose your cool over some miniature teddy bears dressed as members of the Household Cavalry. And you can't afford a watch with inch long diamonds for hands. What you can afford, alas, is some piece of leather tat from the luggagey shop. The luggagey shop, note, is not the actual luggage shop, which sells luggage (hence the name), but the one two doors down which sells things that go on luggage: pointlessly ornate address labels, which would do admirably as bindings for early copies of the Gutenberg Bible; combination locks that are so tiny that a bee might break them; money belts that are so fat and bulky that they say to everyone you meet, 'Hi! I'm wearing five million dollars around my waist'. A load of old luggagey toot and completely pointless. What it also is, unfortunately, is a load of luggagey toot that you can afford. Six minutes later you head for your flight with a leather address label, two combination locks, a money belt, a velour inflatable neck cushion that looks like a gay Cumberland sausage, and a set of adaptor plugs that can only be used in Dubai for hair-driers purchased in the Netherlands. Thanks a bundle, luggagey shop.

The luggagey shop, note, is not the actual luggage shop, which sells luggage (hence the name), but the one two doors down which sells things that go on luggage.

AIRPORT 'PUBS' AND 'RESTAURANTS'

∾

Pubs and restaurants are often the focus of the communities that they serve. Admittedly, pubs are more focus-like than restaurants, but restaurants smell nicer and are less likely to offer food that has been pickled and put in a jar. But what they both have in common is that they serve the needs of the people who frequent them. If they don't, they go bust, hence the lack of Pacific Rim fusion cuisine bistros in the Orkneys or indeed sawdust-floored Cockney fighting pubs in Cheshire.

The exceptions to this rule are, as you may have guessed from the heading, airport pubs and restaurants. They continue to exist not because they are much loved and of astonishingly high quality, but because there isn't anywhere else. You can't have a dodgy pint in the Pretend Arms at Heathrow Airport and decide to move on down the road a bit, because there is no road to move on a down bit. You can't have a crappy salad with bits of egg and human hair in at Chez A La Pierre's Frenchesque Restaurant at Manchester International and decide that next time you might opt for a Chinese instead because there isn't a Chinese.

MODERN LIFE

'Sportswear worn by the unfit is vile and unattractive,
like jewellery worn by pigs.'

SPORTS CASUAL

~

Once worn only by fit and healthy athletes, sportswear is now the badge of the unfit, the large and the idle. Sportswear worn by the unfit is vile and unattractive, like jewellery worn by pigs. We don't see our finest athletes dressed in brown trousers held together with string and old jumpers with moths flying out of them, so why do big fat slobs wear sportswear? Easy; because sportswear is stretchy and loose, and so is ideal for concealing rolls of fat and big bums.

Companies like Adidas and Nike pretend to cater for sportspeople, and their ads feature the cream of the world's runners, footballers and basketball players, but in reality most of their customers would suffer a fatal heart attack if they had to bend down and scrabble for the remote amongst the pizza boxes scattered at their fat feet. Honest advertising for sportswear, in fact, would feature enormous people waddling down to the off-licence, sleeping some tinnies off on a burst sofa, and moving one gigantic buttock to let out some stomach gas. Maybe the noise of said stomach gas inspired Nike to call their logo a 'swoosh'. 'Did you just swoosh,' Phil?'. 'No, it was the dog.'

The other annoying thing about sportswear is that it's revolting. It looks like vomit's idea of good clothing. And it doesn't care to mix and match. Wearing the blue hooded top of one brand with the lime green tracksuit pants of another creates an alarming look. Put a big arse in the equation and you have something very frightening indeed.

Not that co-ordinating this stuff helps. David Icke proved this when he began wearing lurid matching shellsuits at the height of his 'Son of God' phase. He cut a distinctive figure, to say the least. A distinctive figure who could be seen from space.

CALL CENTRES
∾

'**H**ello. Thank you for calling Dodgycorp. Your call is very important to us, which is why you are listening to the voice of a woman who got sacked three years ago to be replaced by nine people in Delhi. For security reasons and to give us a good laugh at your continuing frustration, this call will be monitored by teenagers and recorded. If you wish to report a fault, press nine to be transferred to our customer relations department, or, to be honest, a faint hissing sound which will go dead after you have been holding for 20 minutes. If you wish to cancel your account, press seven to listen to a fake ringing tone as no way are we going to make it easy for you to get out of your contract. If you wish to speak to a customer services operative, press three and your call will be transferred to our customer services centre in Bombay. As the operative lives several thousand miles away from where you do, and on the wages we pay her will never be able to share the lifestyle you enjoy, she may have difficulty understanding the nature of your enquiry. But then, as her job consists entirely of reading answers off a piece of paper with the words TEN QUESTIONS THAT CUSTOMERS ALWAYS ASK, she should be all right. Thank you for calling Dodgycorp. This call will now abruptly terminate, its only lingering shadow the amount it cost on your phone bill'.

BANKS

There was a time – a time before memory – when a bank was a benevolent place run by Captain Mainwaring devoted to the safe care of your money. Now banks just exist to give Satan something to do with his spare time. Banks are like open sewers for greed, incompetence and fear. You might as well nail your ears to a telephone and burn your savings: it would save time in the long run. Here are some exhibits for the prosecution:

1) CHARGES. 'We regret we are now compelled to charge for the use of certain facilities'. Compelled by what? Sheer naked greed? You're a bank. You're raking it in. You earn about a million quid an hour. Even Paul McCartney doesn't do that. But then Paul McCartney made his millions providing stuff people actually wanted and enjoyed. He didn't write them a letter saying, 'Owing to the difficulty of writing *Hey Jude*, I am forced to increase my charges.'

2) FREE GIFTS. Hey, instead of a set of piggy banks shaped like pigs or a mousemat with the bank's logo on, how about this for a gift? Ten thousand quid. That'd make people want to bank with you.

3) BANKING HOURS. Banks are, brilliantly, only open when people are at work. The moment you leave work, too late. Bank's been shut for two hours. You'd think, given their so-called financial acumen, banks would be open 24 hours a day. Hey, they don't mind charging

you interest while you sleep, maybe they could let you pay your cheques in after six pm.

4) THEY KEEP TURNING INTO PUBS. Why don't they just cut out the middleman and have banks that serve alcohol? If we were all pissed when we went in, surely we'd try and borrow more money at absurdly high rates. We'd drop change, we'd add cheques up wrongly – banks would be even richer than they are now.

5) PENS ON CHAINS. The chain is always about an inch too short to write with comfortably. And when you do manage to crouch down and scribble something that looks like a signature, there's no ink in the pen. Why not just be common and get a load of cheap tiny biros like in a bookie's?

6) FOREIGN EXCHANGE COUNTER. In the middle of the lunchtime rush, as the queue stretches out of the bank and down the street, one counter is always empty; the foreign exchange one. Who is this bloke? How can he stand to sit there all day, counting Thomas Cook traveller's cheques, when there are people next to him actually serving real customers? Is he some sort of fake bank clerk, who's been put there by M15 to spy on something, or is he just too stupid to cash proper cheques or accept deposits so they give him foreign money to play with?

CASHPOINTS
⁓

These are vile windows of the devil. And that's leaving aside the eejit stood in front of you who's spending an hour staring at the display because a) he doesn't speak enough English to work out what PLEASE SELECT A LANGUAGE FOR THIS TRANSACTION means, or b) the cashpoint won't give him any money and he thinks if he stares at it long enough, it will start crying tenners. Cashpoints are awful things. Here are some of their tricks.

1) Eating the card. It's not your card, bankboy. Give it back or next time I see you I'll take your cashcard and make you eat it.

2) Taunting messages. Whenever the cashpoint tells you, 'YOU HAVE INSUFFICIENT FUNDS,' its next message is invariably, 'THINKING OF BUYING A HOUSE?' This is deliberate.

3) 'This bank will not charge you for using the cashpoint.' Well, whoop de doop. Do you want a medal? 'This bank will not pour molten lava into your ear.' Same thing.

4) 'CLOSED WHILE WE UPDATE OUR RECORDS.' What the hell are you talking about? We've got computers, we know that updating records takes about fourteen seconds. 'CLOSED WHILE WE LOOK AT DONKEY PORN,' more like.

MEETINGS

T he biggest waste of time since King Canute tried to turn back the Millennium Dome. In theory, meetings are there so that like-minded executives or 'creatives' can get together and thrash out a plan. In practice, they are an excuse for people with no skills other than sitting in a room, eating sandwiches and talking cack to show off.

Meetings last for hours when generally their content can be summed

In practice, they are an excuse for people with no skills other than sitting in a room, eating sandwiches and talking cack to show off.

up on an email written on the back of a walnut shell. They go round in circles, getting nowhere and relying on repetition to kick them off again whenever somebody is about to say, 'Hey, this is utterly futile, and we've run out of coffee.' They are there to disguise the fact that most executives' jobs can be done a) by a drunken pimp and b) in about 20 seconds. This fact can be proven by simply listing standard meetings procedures, all of which are designed to bore the very concept of time itself to a standstill:

1) Reading 'the minutes of the last meeting'. a) 'Minutes' is a misnomer. 'Hours' is better. b) Why? When you buy a car, do you have to tell everyone about the last time you bought a car? Why waste all this time going over what everyone already know? Why not have fun and try and imagine the minutes of the next meeting. 'Item 4. Jeff Chapman confirmed our plans to give every employee a personal jetpack by May. Item 5. Break for food pills.'

2) Flip charts. If your idea is so simple that it can be demonstrated with felt tip pen graphics, maybe you could just tell it to us? Or wouldn't that be time-consuming enough?

3) Conference calls. 'John can't be here today, so he'll be joining us on the speaker link.' That should make the video presentation even more pointless. 'Hi, John, this is Alan. We're looking at some sort of graph now....'

4) Sandwiches. Jesus, how long is this meeting? Why don't we just go out to dinner? Is there a wine list?

5) Site visit. The ultimate weapon. If a meeting has so lost its thread that it is unravelling into a huge rope of waffle, someone will invariably suggest that we 'go and look at the site.' This is a way of taking the meeting outdoors. It's an excuse to put on hard hats and wellington boots, walk around pointing at things, and generally get in the way of some people who are actually doing some work. Oh, and go to lunch afterwards.

6) 'Phil, you've been very quiet.' He's dead.

7) 'Right, good work everyone. Shall we meet up again, same time tomorrow, and go over these points one more time?' DOES ANYONE HAVE A GUN? OR A LENGTH OF ROPE? PILLS! VODKA? ANYTHING!

THE NATIONAL LOTTERY

'It Could Be You,' is their slogan. Statistically speaking, a more accurate slogan would be 'It Couldn't Be You.'

IKEA

Why not save time by smashing up your own furniture and then sending the Swedish embassy a cheque for ten thousand pounds? 'Shopping' at Ikea – or IKEA as they call it, as though it was a cry of pain and not a shop – is a horrible thing. Ikea operates on the assumption that, because they are an 'alternative' to the dull convention of a proper furniture shop, they can get away with murder. Thus everything is laid out according to the design ideas of a toddler; heaps of crap lying everywhere for you to find by hiring a native guide. ('I am Oggo and I will take you to the source of the little lamps with pastel blue shades.') Giant pallets are strewn everywhere, often just as resting places for those hard-to-carry blue bags. Somewhere, someone is selling meatballs to give the place the smell of a small abattoir. A pensioner wanders, lost in the crowd, buffeted by the masses, through the bed section. Two parents are frantically searching for their child in the 'ball room', where it has sunk to the bottom. Some members of staff are staring at a wall, or laughing at a joke, or doing anything to avoid the customer with an enquiry standing all of an inch away.

The whole thing is a mess. Just because we don't want any chintz – and apparently only murderers and nonces do – we are expected to put up with a day in a warehouse for bastards. The very names of the products are annoying, names like Billy and Sigbog, which suggest that every single item in Ikea is named after a Scandinavian village idiot. None of their beds are proper sizes, suggesting that they were made for trolls. And as for assembling the stuff – what's wrong with proper screws? Why don't they want us to use real nuts and bolts? Are conventional hardware products, tried and tested since the building of the pyramids, so threatening that we can't be allowed to have them. 'Why, this screw fits here! And see, it makes the table leg not wobbly! What madness is this?'

SCHOOL REUNIONS
❧

You left school 10, 15, 20 years ago. You have not kept in touch with some or any of your classmates. That's a big clue, right there. Despite many opportunities, like your mum still being friends with some other ex-pupil's mum and your brother getting a job locally, you have consistently and utterly failed to keep in touch with the spotty freaks you vaguely remember from school. Also this is school we're talking about. People you knew at school, not people you met at a three day orgy on top of Table Mountain, or people you met on the first Mars landing. Former school acquaintances.

What kind of person wants to meet people they were at school with anyway? A weirdo, that's who. Or someone who's done quite well since then and wants to boast about it. Maybe someone who hasn't had any fun since they left school and thinks a reunion will bring back happy memories.

It's not likely. Here are the top five things you will find yourself saying at a school reunion:

1) 'Yes, I have put on weight, now you come to mention it. And lost some hair, too. Wow. Good job you brought it up.'
2) 'Did you used to beat me up or did I used to beat you up?'
3) 'Someone I can't remember married someone I've never heard of? Really?'
4) 'So you're the one who locked me in the stationery cupboard for the weekend? How weird, I've got your loan application back in my office.'
5) 'You've brought photos of your car! Gather round, everybody!'

SQUEEGEE BASTARDS
∾

Those people who clean your car window with a bit of filthy crap and then demand money. Instead of giving them money, give them a blast from the high powered water-pistol full of horse urine that you keep in your car.

LANGUAGE PEDANTS
∾

These people are generally from abroad and have a real downer on loan words. Loan words are words from one language that appear in another language. Thus they are bog all to do with loans.

'Hello, is that the Dictionnaire Anglais-Francais?'
'Oui.'
'Ah good, this is the Oxbridge English Dictionary. Um, I don't quite know how to put this, but a couple of years ago, we lent you some words.'
'What of eet?'

'Well, they were quite new. Brand new. 'Internet', that was one.
'Broadband', that was another. And we didn't get them back.'
   'Ah! We are still using zem.'
'Well, it's not just those, you know. You said you only wanted 'weekend'
for a couple of days, and we've not heard hide nor hair of 'camping' for
decades.'

The French have that Académie française thing where they try to vet
words before they enter the language. In much the same way, presumably, that King Canute tried to vet the sea before it came onto
the beach. You can't stop it, mate. It's historical inevitability.

But the really sad linguistic thing is making words look like they were
out of your own language in the first place. 'Taxi' in Welsh is 'Tacsi', written
that way, as Kingsley Amis remarked, for the benefit of Welsh people who've
never seen an X before. In Ukrainian, the word for 'haircut' is 'herkut'. The weirdest one of all is the Maltese
word 'xemindifer' which sounds really exotic and means 'railway'. It's
nicked, ironically, from the French word for railway, 'chemin de fer'.
Which, by the way, means 'way of iron' and is another typically crap
roundabout way of saying something sensible like railway.

In Ukrainian, the word for 'haircut' is 'herkut'

SPLIT INFINITIVES
~

This won't take long. The notion that the split infinitive is gram-
matically wrong is based on Old English grammar books, which
took their rules of grammar from Latin, whether they were applica-
ble to English or not. Latin is a language where infinitives can't be
split because they're one word, like 'esse' or 'amare', and so the reason
you don't split infinitives in Latin is because you can't. But in
English, you can. And in English, of course, if you can do it, generally you do do it.

So if another pillock in a tweed jacket with leather patches starts banging out about split infinitives, ask the dusty old tossbadger *why* they are bad. Like an actual reason? Like, do they sound bad? Do they cause disease? Or is it just the only weapon you have in your sad empty mothy old pretend professor existence to beat people up with who have actual real life lives to live? And you can know where you can stick 'never ending a sentence with a preposition' up into.

BUSINESS WORDS
∼

When you travel on a train, you are a customer, not a passenger. This is because passengers are people who have got onto a train to travel somewhere, and a person who does that clearly has no business being on a train nowadays. Customer is a much better word, as it just means someone who has bought something which may be good or bad or a complete tossing waste of money like a train ticket. Customers used to be people who, apparently, were always right, which is a neat trick. ('How can we decide which of these two women is the real mother of this baby? Shall we ask King Solomon?' 'No, a customer's just come in. Let's ask him.') But then everyone became a customer and the whole thing got out of hand, perhaps because not everyone can be right.

Similarly, around this time, there were other linguistic developments. In the early 1990s Radio One DJs were suddenly told to refer to the station they broadcast on as 'One FM', just in case some listeners were allergic to the word 'radio', or maybe the BBC reckoned they could trick the listeners into thinking they were watching some kind of special tiny television with very, very limited visuals. The word 'client' shifted in meaning. There are only two groups of people who use this phrase regularly to describe their customers; lawyers and prostitutes. 'Active' was replaced by 'pro-active', as though the word pro was Latin for 'very'. 'Facilitator' came in, a word that in Latin does mean 'person who makes something easy' but in English means 'person who makes something easy very complicated and difficult'.

TRAINS

'The buffet cart will go up and down the train in a half-hearted sort of way, blocking the aisles so that people who want the toilet or even to get off at Doncaster will be trapped for hours.'

THE RAILWAYS

An area that would reduce even the meekest of all the saints to a blood-boiling, enraging, hair-tearing, blaspheming, sandal-throwing human jelly. Anyone reading this who is in a senior railway management position should really be off doing something more useful instead, like throwing a rope over a beam or nailing their buttocks to a railway line. A railway line, by the way, in a different country. There's no point doing it here; there aren't any bastard trains.

There was a time before the railways were privatised and everyone used to bitch about them and how they were inefficient and late and the food was rubbish – ironic, eh? Because while we don't have so many rails strikes any more, everything else about the railways is completely appalling (and the reason we don't have rail strikes is we don't have any unions any more, unless things like the Worshipful Guild Of Lacemakers, Buttonhole-Sewers and Braid Braiders count, which they don't).

Nowadays, not only is the national rail network cut into tiny fiefdoms like the Duchy of Fatcatland and the Grand Palatinate of Some Blokes Who Used To Own A Chain Of Bookie's, so that if you want to do something as outrageously 19th century as actually plan your journey, you need 56 timetables and a friend in Carlisle. A simple journey to Devon can be a nightmare, if you miss the train from Paddington run by Great South-Western Incompetent But At Least Vaguely Direct Trains and end up going from Waterloo with

Southern-Westerly Where In The Name Of All The Demons Of Hell Are We Railways. For once upon a time the trains were run by dull men in Two Ronnies glasses whose idea of a good time was to introduce a scary sort of gay SS uniform for British Rail workers to wear, but now the trains are run by people who shouldn't be allowed to organise a raffle. A raffle with one ticket in it. And no prizes.

The same goes for the track company, only more so. Because, not content with selling off the actual trains, someone had the bright idea of selling off the actual stuff the trains go up and down on. Separately.

So the people who are responsible for the trains and the people who are responsible for the track are not the same. This means that when there is a train wreck no-one is there to take the blame. And let's be honest here, train wrecks are a sadly frequent occurrence. How far we have come since the evil days of nationalisation and state responsibility, eh?

TRAIN CARRIAGES
∾

Three little words – 'are now useless'. In the old days, train carriages were the last vestiges of civilised public transport. They had doors and smoking sections and they only seated five or six people. Everyone kept themselves to themselves, preferably by hiding behind the biggest newspaper in the world (newspapers in the old days were so big that either they must have had astonishingly detailed news stories or else the photos were bloody massive). And the greatest fun to be had was in pretending that there were no free seats.

'Excuse me, is this seat taken?'

'I sorry, me Polish. Also have infectious disease. Zzchoo!'

Never failed. But now there aren't any train carriages, except on some of the much, much older branch lines. There are just coaches. Row upon row of seats, some with tables, some without, and some with a weird space in front so that people with 25 pieces of luggage can store them there and trip the elderly. There is no privacy whatever, unless you want to spend the whole journey in the revolting toilet. Oh, and there is a coach or carriage labelled QUIET COACH, which is shorthand for COACH FULL OF PEOPLE WHO TUT

IF YOU EVEN RUSTLE YOUR NEWSPAPER. These are, incidentally, the same people who will stand in front of you in any queue talking complete drivel about their unendingly dull lives to an underpaid counter hand. But answer one phone call and the air is thick with palates being clicked.

TRAIN STAFF

Once upon a time all train staff were jolly Mister Porters whose duties were threefold; hoicking great big cabin trunks around for wee public schoolboys home for the summer vac, making sure that no-one put their heads out of the window, and

blowing whistles a bit too often. Then came nationalisation and they became BR staff, moody, strike-prone and with an attitude to the concept of buffet cars that would have been the envy of any Moscow shop-owner. ('Sandwiches, sir?' We don't have any. In fact, there ain't no such thing. You must have invented 'em.') BR staff were bad-tempered, rude and with all the fierce independence of Mujaheddin. This could not last. After privatisation, or as pedants probably call it, 're-privatisation' (see PEDANTS), railway staff became a strange bunch.

Part actual person who works on a train, part unnecessary customer services operative, they no longer seem to know who they are. Are they a proud tribe who once blew whistles a bit too often and revelled in the sudden clatter of a metal grille in a buffet car? Or are they pointless nerks in cheap suits who want us to fill in customer 'surveys' and drink 'free' coffee (free with every £450 first class ticket, that is – you might as well save money by fitting an engine on a coffee cup and driving that to Luton instead).

One day train staff will hear the distant hoot of a loco whistle and remember their origins, roaming free in packs across railway stations and depots across the land. And they will tear their stupid name badges from their nasty Dralon blouses, rise up as one and say, 'Now if you'd been here half an hour ago, we did have pork pies.' In the meantime, they continue to be annoying in, well, annoying ways. It's all part of the bigger picture. These days you don't know where you are with the railways. Often literally.

RESERVED SEATS ON TRAINS

All the seats on trains have a little bit of cardboard on the back in a specially-designed and built slot that says something like: BRISTOL – JOHN O'GROATS ONE WAY. They are, oddly for something bureaucratic, clearly labelled. So it's not too weird that if you see a seat with a tag that says BRISTOL – JOHN O'GROATS, and the train has just pulled out of Bristol, you might assume that the seat is now not going to be sat in. Don't.

All reserved seats on trains are Shrödinger's Seats. They get this name from the famously mystifying physics theory known as Shrödinger's Cat. No-one who isn't a physicist really understands this theory, but it appears to hang on the notion that if you put a cat in a box with a radioactive isotope, if one particular thing happens, the cat will be dead when you open the box. And if another thing happens, it won't. Spectacular nonsense, obviously, which goes a long way to explaining why physicists are rarely allowed to own cats. But it does work when applied to reserved seats on trains.

All reserved seats on trains are Shroedinger's Seats. They get this name from the famously mystifying physics theory known as Shroedinger's Cat.

Here's how it goes down. Our traveller, weary from seeing the Clifton Suspension Bridge and the SS Great Britain and Massive Attack and all the other fine sights of Bristol, sees the reserved seat with no-one in it. He has two courses of action:

1) 'Neat!' he thinks, and plonks himself down into it, arranging his many CDs and paperback books around himself for the journey. And immediately he does so – a mad-eyed squaddie from the Wirral called Spug appears from the buffet car with fourteen cans of lager, and suggests in special short words that our traveller go somewhere, and have sex with himself in several equally special ways.

2) But! If our traveller, experienced in the ways of men, thinks, 'Nah – a reserved seat, however empty, is still reserved,' and spends the rest of the journey to John O'Groats sitting on his luggage in the corridor while people spill coffee on him, then the theory of Shrödinger's

Seat guarantees that no-one will claim the seat, and it will remain empty for the rest of the journey.

This is also, incidentally, the reason why physicists always nab the best seats on trains.

FIRST CLASS

~

Designed solely to annoy anyone who's spending the entire journey standing up in the buffet car or sitting on their luggage in the corridor. There are three empty carriages right behind you. The Russian Revolution was begun for less. (For revenge, see PEOPLE WHO HAVEN'T BOUGHT A WEEKEND SAVER).

TRAIN FOOD

~

All stand-up comedians and radio personalities before 1980 had one train food gag – curly sandwiches. They were obsessed with the fact that British Rail served the oldest sandwiches known to man.

How audiences howled as some fat fool in a frilly shirt made jokes about sandwiches that predated the pyramids or contained fragments of the True Cross. But notice, they only ever went on about the sandwiches. In those days, the rest of the food, though basic, was perfectly fine. True, the average contents of a BR buffet were:

245 packets of salt and vinegar crisps

500 Tunnock's Marshmallow Things

47 Marathon bars

689 cans of Irn Bru

2 cans of shandy

and a pork pie in some sort of mould toupée

but they were all the average passenger wanted (apart from the pork pie, which now lives with a family of sardine fishermen in Kent). Visit a buffet car now and what do you get? A load of crap, that's what.

For some reason, it was decided that the contents of train buffets should go a bit up-market. But, as buffet cars can't actually ever be up-market, since they are in fact sideways tin cafes that run out of stock before Milton Keynes three times a day, this was clearly a plan doomed from the meeting of flipwits (see MEETINGS) that hatched it. The food now served in buffet cars is a half-hearted attempt to copy the work of some of the more incompetent celebrity chefs (see CELEBRITY CHEFS).

In fact the food may actually be made from the recipes that never made it into the TV cookbooks; certainly a lot of it would qualify for

The food now served in buffet cars is a

halfhearted attempt to copy the work of some

of the more incompetent celebrity chefs

inclusion in books with names like Jamie's Potentially Fatal Kitchen or Nigella's Inedible Slop Bites. The average contents of a modern buffet car are:

- **15 lemon sole tikka masalas**
(microwave until sauce is boiling but rice still plasticy)

- **43 packets of something that on the box looks a bit Mexican but inside looks like hot sick**

- **472 rocket and medallions de veau sandwiches (none sold since 1983)**

- **321 'breakfast baps' (bread rolls so hot they will spontaneously combust in your mouth before releasing a molten stream of egg yolk down your throat)**

- **556 little bottles of Cabernet Solihull 2003**

- **556 little bottles of Vin De White Stuff**

- **76 Snickers bars (née Marathon)**

- **2 cans of Kestrel.**

BUFFET TROLLEYS

∾

'Hi! We can't be bothered to open the buffet car, owing to either alcoholism among management or a dropping-the-key-down-a-drain accident earlier in the week. This means that most of the food we normally stock, execrable though it is, is currently not available. And in fact our stock is so small that it can all be fitted onto some sort of shopping trolley.

The buffet cart will go up and down the train in a half-hearted sort of way, blocking the aisles so that people who want the toilet or even to get off at Doncaster will be trapped for hours, until we completely run out of our meagre supply of provisions. At which point, we will do one more run up and down the train, just to rub it in. And then serve an enormous feast of roasted pig's face in sherry gravy to all our passengers in First Class. This feast will be broadcast over the tannoy. That is all.'

VIRGIN TRAINS
✑

Whatever else Richard Branson has done, he will live forever in public infamy for his Virgin Train service. You would think that a man who had made a good fist of running an international airline – something that is quite hard to do, probably – might be in with a chance of running a railway efficiently. Certainly none of his planes are ever three hours late into Los Angeles International Airport or have no sandwiches in Business Class or spend an afternoon standing outside Doncaster smelling of cabbage.

It's a fair bet that Branson's jumbo jets do not have overflowing toilets and that when you ask for some duty-free Scotch, the hostess will not say, 'We haven't got any, here's a can of Kestrel instead'. Why, it's as though in the world of international airlines, Virgin are in hot competition with hundreds of other companies and have to be good and efficient to survive. Whereas in the world of national railways, they can do what they like because no-one else wants the job, and their only competition is Thomas the Tank Engine, who can only go as far as Budleigh Salterton before he has to have a lie-down.

Similarly, let's not forget that Richard Branson made his millions not from trains but from his Virgin Records record company. Remember them, they belong to EMI or Daimler now, but back in the day, Virgin's weird logo of two Siamese twins in the nudd was a guarantee of musical quality. Actually it wasn't, it was a guarantee of some appalling hippy tosh with a 14-minute moog synthesiser solo taking the high ground on side four, but that's not the point. Virgin Records was a successful, popular business.

Mind you, it's unlikely it would have done well if WH Smith ran out of Mike Oldfield albums and instead handed out little forms that said, 'We apologise for the non-arrival of *Tubular Bells*. This is due to slightly distorted guitars at Harpenden. Please accept this voucher for five pence instead.'

OCCUPATIONS

'The Guinness Book of Records doesn't tell you is who holds the record for World's Most Hated Profession. But they don't have to; everybody knows. It's estate agents.'

ESTATE AGENTS
~

The Earth does not actually have a scum on it, because it's a planet not a pond. But if it did, that scum would be made of estate agents. Fizzing, frothing, bubbling, talking swampgas out of every orifice, estate agents have been around pretty much for ever. As long as language itself, really. The oldest word in the English language, significantly, is 'land'. This is true; it's in the 1970 edition of the *Guinness Book of Records* and they'd know. What the 1970 edition of the *Guinness Book of Records* doesn't tell you is who holds the record for World's Most Hated Profession. But they don't have to; everybody knows. It's estate agents (or, as they call them in America, 'realtors', which might be short for 'real tossers').

Estate agents exist solely to make money out of a situation where a third party ought not to even be involved, let alone be making money. Here's how it used to be:

'Good evening, sirrah. I was admiring your thatched cottage with original Tudor features and I wondered, might you wish to sell it?'

> *'Why, my good fellow! I was just about to put it on the market. See, I have made a wooden sign with FOR FALE written on it in olden lettering.'*

'How much do you think your humble abode is worth?'

> *'Well, let's see, it's quite large and there's a nice garden full of*

roses and truffles, but on the downside it smells of pigs and it's built over a plague pit. I'd say – 40 florins.'

'I'll give you 30. I've just noticed there aren't any windows.'

'Done. Let me put my meagre belongings and this pig into a handcart and the place is yours.'

Simple, eh? So what happened? It's hard to say, but probably at some point in the 17th century (which was a great time for documents and witnessing things and saw the final withering away of feudalism and that), somebody thought, 'Hang on, this selling my cottage business is way too easy, and besides land is a valuable commodity, almost as valuable as potatoes,' and decided to balls it all up.

Before you know it, selling your own house direct is considered a bit weird, like selling your daughter in the market square, and estate agents become richer than anyone else in the world. You can't phone the other person in the deal because this makes the estate agent ratty. Why? Because it more than gently suggests that the estate agent is in fact completely unnecessary. Imagine buying a pair of shoes via some sort of shoe agent:

'Hi, I'd like to buy these shoes.'

'I'm afraid we're selling them via a shoe agent. I'll get him to call you on Monday and he can show you round the shoes.'

'But I want them now. Can't I just buy them off you?'

'No, it's best if the shoe agent does it. He's got some very good descriptions of shoes, you know. Look at this one – 'excellent laces, with south-facing heel and own uppers'.

It'd be slightly better if estate agents understood just what sub-aquatic lowlifes they were. But they don't. They go round in cheap suits and nasty small cars. (Why don't estate agents ever have big cars? And what is it with minis and estate agents? Are they trying to get us to think estate agent = criminal via some mental association of minis and *The Italian Job*?) Oh, and they take mobile phone calls whenever you're with them, just to show how important they are, and whenever you go into their office the first thing they say is, 'I'm just going to lunch, Susan', like anyone cares, particularly Susan, who knows that 'lunch' probably means half a bottle of vodka in the living room of the showhouse on the new estate.

Estate agents are about as honest as politicians, they've helped materially to drive up property prices so high that only a first time monarch could buy a flat, let alone a first time buyer, and, perhaps significantly, they have their own language of lies.

ESTATE-AGENTESE

SOME RENOVATION NECESSARY – 20 years ago. 'Some demolition necessary' more like it.

NO CHAIN INVOLVED – owners fled country years ago.

IMPOSING – not the house, but your debts if you buy it.

STUDIO – from the Latin, meaning 'I cannot breathe.'

ORIGINAL FEATURES – open sewer, Indian burial ground, gateway into Hell, etc.

HANDY FOR SHOPPING – you can buy drugs outside your own front door.

HAS CHARACTER – only if that character is in *Paradise Lost*, and has horns.

… what is it with

minis and estate

agents?

HAIRDRESSERS

∾

Hairdressers are rude, snooty, bad-mannered and act as though they were the sole heirs to the throne of 18th-century France, when in actual fact they are generally people who couldn't get into stage school and are secretly hoping that one day someone famous will come in to get a haircut and give them a part in their new movie. The fact that Steven Spielberg is unlikely to come to Romford and demand the worst haircut of his life never seems to occur to them.

Hairdressers would all rather be working on women's coiffeur than men's barnets. Women are, hair-wise, a lot more adventurous than men. They've also generally got more hair than men, and they keep it for more years. Completely fair, but for a man visiting a hairdresser, there is always that sense that you have strolled into the wrong emporium altogether. Hairdressers are not barbers. They do not sell johnnies. They rarely put human flesh into pies. And none of them have ever been surgeons. Despite this, they put on extraordinary airs.

'Do you have an appointment?'

    'No. I want a haircut, not an interview with the Dalai Lama.'

'You have to have an appointment.'

    'Oh. Well, maybe that man there, the one reading a magazine, could get off his arse and cut my hair.'

'Darren's on his break.'

That is another thing about hairdressers. Walk past a barbershop and they are busy chopping off locks like there's no tomorrow. It's a veritable General Motors assembly line of follicle devastation. Walk past your local hairdressers and invariably only one of them will be actually cutting some actual hair. The other six will be:

a) reading a magazine in a chair

b) shrieking with laughter and throwing their heads back.

c) drinking lots of wine.

Hairdressers cannot get to the end of the day without breaking out the wine. They must all be rat-arsed by going home time, and woe betide the poor sod who's got the 5.55 haircut appointment. He or she is going home looking like the sexual partner of a damaged echidna.

BUILDERS
∾

Given that their name contains the word 'build', you might think they would do some actual building. 'Breaker' is a better word, as generally they manage not only to smash up the things they said they'd have to smash up, but also a few they didn't, like your cistern, and your furniture.

Reliable? Hiring a wolf and expecting it to be round on Monday morning at eight would be more sensible, and less dangerous. Builders understand the word 'quotation' in its literary sense, i.e. 'an extract from a greater whole', as their idea of a quote is just a small part of the terrible crippling sum that will later be presented to you. They have to be stood over while they work, like toddlers, otherwise they go off and do something else. Generally that something else will be doing building work at someone else's house.

You can't go on holiday when they're there, otherwise in your absence your home will become a kind of doss house for incompetents. On returning, your home will have turned into something that resembles the aftermath of a teenage party – beer cans everywhere, broken windows, stains on the carpet, and a huge boy called Ginger flat out sparko on the living-room carpet.

DENTISTS
∾

The book and movie *Marathon Man* posited the not entirely absurd hypothesis that dentists might actually be senior Nazi torturers on the run. In retrospect, this seems a little too soft on some dentists, as it gives them motivation. Most dentists revel in the combination of causing pain and charging for it that their jobs give them.

Dentist's surgeries used to be sensible places, given that their purpose was purely to cause pain and misery. Nowadays, however, they're all tarted up. They play classical music, which is allegedly to put you at your ease, but really just makes you think of that bit in *A Clockwork Orange* where they put metal things in Malcolm McDowell's eyes and made him listen to Classic FM. They have tasteful posters of Van Gogh paintings, to remind you that insanity often leads to mutilation. And then they set to it. Where once they just used to go at you with a pair of pliers, now they have to turn your mouth into a kind of miniature building site. Wires, clamps, pipes, wadding – even if your teeth wanted to run for it, they couldn't. Then the injections. Injections are ingenious; they're supposed to reduce pain, but in reality they actually cause it (see WHEEL CLAMPS). And they never work, thus allowing your dentist to inject more and more anaesthetic into your already novocaine-addled jaws. And then, as you're lying there, mouth full of miniature scrap, gums feeling like so much porridge, the dentist will try and start a conversation with you. He may not actually say, 'Is it safe?' but his questions will be equally annoying and unanswerable.

The thing is, dentistry is an overrated profession. They give you all this guff about how they have to train as doctors first, to make you think that dentists actually are doctors. If they really were doctors, they'd be working in a grim health centre and wearing nasty tweed jackets with the elbows missing. Instead, they're working in an opulent Georgian house built on the innocent gums of suffering people (not literally, obviously, a house built on gums wouldn't stay up very long). But they're not. In the end, all dentists are is vets for teeth.

ASTROLOGERS
∾

One of the most annoying lines in aged films and sitcoms is where some old twit says, 'Astrologer, not astronomer, there is a difference,' as though people in real life ever got them mixed up. Yes, it must be pretty hard to tell a man in a white coat holding a telescope and a degree in physics apart from some pillock in a turban with a fake ruby in it. Astronomers and astrologers are completely different. One is a person who maps the movement of the stars via science, mathematics and telescopes. The other is a person who maps the movement of the stars via join-the-dots pictures of bulls and centaurs and fish and then makes up a load of rubbish about it. Astronomers got man onto the Moon. Astrologers would have had man take the day off because it was a bad week to undertake a long journey. Astronomers have mapped the farthest reaches of the galaxy. Astrologers have mapped the farthest reaches of some woman in a soap opera's love life. They are about as comparable as developing the latest nanobyte spy satellite technology and thumping the telly when it's gone on the blink during *Grandstand*.

Astrologers are, pun intended, a waste of space. Their central belief is that what we do is pre-ordained by the alignment of the planets when we are born. This suggests that major heavenly bodies like the planet Jupiter – big, gassy thing with a mole – have nothing better to do than

. . . a person who maps the movement of the stars via join-the-dots pictures of bulls and centaurs and fish and then makes up a load of rubbish about it.

hover over the cot of, say, Barry Grahams from Uttoxeter and go, 'Born 5.35 on a Tuesday morning, eh? He's going to be a greengrocer with a thing for ginger men.' This is not terribly likely. Jeff Wayne, in his concept album *War Of The Worlds*, observed that 'the chances of anything coming from Mars are a million to one/They said'. Which means, in all honesty, that the chances of Mars itself taking an active interest in the doings of one-twelfth of the Earth's population are even more slender.

Then there's stars. These were conveniently lumped together by the ancient Greeks into constellations. Constellations like Pisces and Sagittarius and Capricorn are central to astronomy, because of the Zodiac, which is just a sort of football team of constellations (with Aries on the bench). But constellations might as well be the olden days word for 'a bunch of stars that are sort of next to each other and have no other connection' because that's what they are. You can tell they invented constellations in the days before telescopes because they bear not the slightest resemblance to their names. The ancient Greeks must have named them all after a particularly heavy session on the ouzo, because looking up into the night sky, the casual observer's first thought on seeing a constellation is generally, 'No way is that a bear,' or 'Oh, it's a hunter because those stars are his belt. Well, why don't they call it Orion the Belt with some stars hanging around it.' Even when they get an obvious one, they cock it up. There's a constellation up there with five stars in, three at the top, two at the bottom. Everyone who's ever seen it says, 'Oh look, a giant W'. Not your ancient Greeks. They said, 'Blimey, it's a beautiful maiden chained to a rock,' and called it Cassiopea.

Patent nonsense, then. But this patent nonsense is the foundation and cornerstone of astrology, a word which is derived from the Latin, meaning 'non-science based on pretending that some stars that look like a W look like a beautiful girl chained to a rock.'

Astrologers! They're not even real gypsies.

TRAFFIC WARDENS

~

Last year, traffic wardens sent tickets to a combine harvester in Norfolk, which had supposedly been parked in a London mews, and to an Aberdeen milk float, which was magically parked in Pall Mall. They have even put a ticket on some scaffolding in Glasgow, which is genius. These people are devils. If they could get in your car and wait for you, they would. If they could speed up time so the meter expires, they would. If they could ticket pedestrians for standing... well, you get the picture.

Traffic wardens are, for people whose job consists of standing around in the rain all day getting slagged off by motorists, utterly devoted to their work. So devoted that sometimes you suspect they get given a thousand pounds for ever car they ticket. Either that, or their parents were eaten by a car when they were young and in the orphanage they swore revenge on all vehicles.

TRAFFIC POLICE

Traffic police spend all their time putting cones on the motorway after a car accident, the better to slow down the traffic flow. This brings to mind the phrase 'shutting the stable door after the horse has crashed into the back of a lorry.' It also misses a trick; they don't need to slow the traffic down as every blood-lusting freak who ever bought a Skoda is driving past the wreckage at 15mph, gawping and hoping for severed heads. This is when you want motorway tolls – every accident should have its own Pay-Per-View lane.

ROYALTY

∾

Hey, if you don't like 'em, don't vote for 'em! Kings and queens really are the filth of the galaxy, bullies who've done well. Nip into your local bookshop and have a look at the History section, with particular reference to the kings and queens bit. A good way of whiling away an hour or so is going through the various rulers of this sceptred isle and rating them as per their rap sheet. So instead, say, of that old

'WILLIE, WILLIE, HARRY, STEE, HARRY, DICK, JOHN, HARRY THREE'

or whatever the list of monarchs was that they don't make you learn any more in case you find out how badly your country has been run and for whose benefit – um, instead of doing that list, do this one

'MURDERER, MURDERER, WARMONGER, SERIAL ADULTERER, CHILD MURDERER, WIFE MURDERER, SERIAL KILLER, THIEF, SYPHILITIC, SYPHILITIC, CHINLESS GERMAN, MURDERER, MURDERER, KAISER'S COUSIN, NAZI...'

and so on. Much more fun.

And isn't it funny how we're always complaining about the Hitlers and the Saddams of this world, but give a murdering, torturing, unelected tyrant a gold hat with diamonds on, and we're all curtseying. Here are some of the most spleen-burstingly annoying things that people say in defence of royalty.

1) 'They can't answer back.'

Prince Philip's racist opinions, Chas the Hippy on architecture and farming, the Queen's Speech... Can't answer back? Won't shut up, more like.

2) 'They're ambassadors for this country.'

We've already got lots of ambassadors for this country. They're called 'ambassadors'.

3) 'They're a great advert for this country.'

What exactly would this advert say?

> COME TO BRITAIN! LAND OF RICH CHINLESS
> FORMER GERMANS!
>
> PLEASE VISIT OUR CASTLES AND PALACES!
> THEN GO HOME.
> THEY'RE OURS AND YOU CAN'T HAVE THEM!
>
> THANK YOU FOR ADMIRING OUR ROYAL EVENT.
> YOUR FINANCIAL CONTRIBUTION
> WILL ALMOST OFFSET THE COST
> OF KEEPING THIS FAMILY OF FANCY-DRESSED
> GERMANS IN DIAMONDS AND BEER

4) 'We're the envy of other countries who don't have royalty.'

Yes we are. Other countries would love to have a royal family but for some reason they've never got round to actually getting one. Perhaps they're a bit lazy that way. Or perhaps they can think of more useful ways to spend the money. Like burning it in the town square. Oddly, there are other countries with royalty and they're not the envy of anyone, except possibly the odd cycling club with regal ambitions.

5) 'They're something to look up to.'

Ha ha! Ha! Ha ha ha ha! Even when they were something to look up, they weren't really. They were at it like knives with servant girls, gambling, drinking and taking heroin during the coronation. Probably.

6) 'What would we replace them with?'
Nothing. Or lifesize cheese sculptures of themselves. 'When Prince Charles goes rancid, 'tis summertime.'

'CHUGGERS' – THE CHARITY MUGGERS
❧

Charity collecting used to be a wonderful thing. It consisted entirely of two things:

1) A nice old person rattling a tin outside the library on a Saturday morning who, if you gave him money, would give you a flag on a pin.

2) A fibreglass replica of a Labrador or a boy in calipers with a hole in it to put money in.

Oh, and there was also a pub version of number 2 which was a model lifeboat that you rolled a penny into and it 'launched' into a sea of other pennies. That was charity collecting at its most magnificent. Simple, effective and, in the case of the flag on a pin or the lifeboat, even moderately entertaining. And then someone in a marketing department, some Christopher Biggins-faced divcompoop, decided that charity could be jazzed up and dragged into the 20th century.

See the student in the tabard. See him or her approach you. See them smile, bigly. See them say something at astonishing speed as they step into your path.

'Hellowouldyoubeinterestedinhelpingoutacharity?'

> *'Sorry, I'm in a bit of a – '*

'It won't take a minute.'

> *'All right. Even though you are clearly lying and it will take all day, since you are standing in my way and it would be unseemly for me to push you into traffic, please set out your stall.'*

'We're collecting for blah blah and our aim is blah blah blah to blah in blah and blah.'

> *'I see. That sounds appalling. But I put some money in a fibreglass dog in 1997. I thought that would sort it out.'*

And say what you like about highwaymen, pirates and muggers, they never stood there boring the face off you with a long-winded justification of their cause, they just stuck something in your ribs and told you to hand it over (and let's face it, a pirate's explanation of what he was going to spend your doubloons on would be a sod of a sight more interesting that a charity's administration plans for the next five years).

Oh, and you know what the worst thing is? The reason they're so obsessed with their charity? Because they're getting paid. Yes, unlike your old dear or your fibreglass dog, these people are on a wage. They get ten pounds an hour. And a further portion of your donation goes to the company who employs them. No wonder they have a special nickname – 'Chuggers'. As in 'charity muggers'. Charity muggers are

not street hoods who rob you then give all the dosh to Oxfam, they're students in tabards. Hence the pushiness. And said pushiness works.

In time even the hardest granite can be worn away by the sheer constant pressure of dead air, and, to make sure that you might get to your next appointment, or even home, before the universe gives up the ghost, you find yourself saying:

'All right, look, shut up, it sounds like a good cause, please stop talking. I'll give you some money, dear God, can you actually close your mouth, here, look, a tenner.'

> *'Oh no, sir. I'm not actually collecting money for charity.'*

'What, you're a paid bore?'

> *'No! I'm here actually to persuade people to set up a direct debit. That is, each month a sum of money would be transferred from your account to ours and – '*

'I know what a direct debit is, I'm not a cat. So what you're telling me is you want me to stand here in the street and give you all my bank details – '

> *'Yes but – '*

' – even though we've never met and will never meet again and the ID you've just produced wouldn't convince a lenient tramp – '

> *'It's a student railcard!'*

' – and then every month you'll take money from my account and I get nothing in return but the vague satisfaction that one derives from helping pay a charity administrator's wages – '

> *'You also get a free newsletter, a glossy monthly magazine and a charity catalogue.'*

'All of which cost more to compile, produce, and mail out than the amount of money I plan to give you.'

> *'So you don't want to contribute?'*

'Sod it, I'm blind drunk. Hand me the form.'

See? That's how they get you.

FOURTH RATE 'SPORTING FIGURES'

∼

A major sporting nation? Us? We are the Liechtenstein of sport. Tierra del Fuego could give us a battering and they're an uninhabited island. So we compensate for our utter crapness by 'supporting the underdog'. Very noble, but our sportsmen aren't the underdog, they're under the underdog. And not even closely under the underdog, more working in a coal mine at the centre of the earth that the underdog happens to be walking over.

And as for the last proper thing we won – the 1966 World Cup – well, any Football League side that hadn't won anything since 1966 would be on the dole. England? They're the Accrington Stanley of world soccer. Only less loved.

'D' LIST CELEBRITIES

∼

Famous for being famous? Famous for being worthless wastes of oxygen, skin, bone and hair more like. D list celebrities are so numerous and so... space-taking-up... that we should find new uses for them, like sandbags or ballast. What balloon journey would not be improved by the knowledge that, in order to get a bit higher, in a few minutes you will have to throw Jeremy Spake over the side?

Reality TV, celebrity magazines, TV talking heads... as you may have heard, Andy Warhol once said that in the future people would be famous for 15 minutes. Actually, what he may have said was, 'In the future people will be famous for sod all.' Fame, as a concept, is clearly over. Like rockabilly, ancient Sumeria and the Sinclair ZX80, fame is an idea whose time has been and gone.

Consider this; there was a time when being famous was extremely hard to achieve. There was no TV or cinema, no radio, no cameras, nothing. Most well-known folk were recognisable by their shields, or by their portraits, neither of which looked much like them – one being a picture of a red lion, the other being a picture of a man with a flat face bending his head slightly. To be famous, you had to be king.

And now, thanks to TV and magazines and films, we have people who are famous for doing bog all. People who are on TV because they were in a TV series. Never mind people who are famous for being famous, nowadays we have people who are famous for not being famous. We have TV non-entities interviewing other TV non-entities on the subject of TV shows featuring TV non-entities. TV ate itself a long time ago, and now we are just watching the results.

MAGICIANS

Magicians can't do magic. This, sadly, is one of the sad facts of life, like there not being a Santa Claus, or X-ray glasses not actually enabling you to see women naked under their clothes. Magicians do tricks. They start off with a kit when they're about seven, and spend Christmas Day boring the pants off relatives with some bits of plastic and elastic bands and some obviously fake playing cards. This is the point when most of us jack in the magicianship thing and start to think seriously about accountancy as a profession.

Magicians, however, keep going, learning more tricks, buying more impressive capes and eventually hitting puberty, when they somehow convince themselves that girls will fancy them if they do magic. No, Mephisto the Spotabulous, you've confused 'magician' with 'musician'. Girls like hairy lads who play guitars and wear their hair long and their jeans too close for comfort. They don't like slightly plump boys in capes and bowties who invite you to their room and then apparently try to suffocate a rabbit in a top hat. Magicians are, in fact, nerds who fancy themselves, sort of pre-computer geeks who go on about the romance of the theatre when really they just mean the romance of losing one's virginity.

If the idea of magicians isn't annoying enough, there's the actuality. Sometimes in life you will be made to go and see a magician. True, if they're good, you won't be able to work out how they did it. But, and here's the point, *you don't care how they did it.* You know they didn't actually saw a woman in half or make a tiger vanish, so it must have been some dull combination of woodwork and physics. The explanation, if one ever comes, will be both boring and complicated and afterwards you still won't care. Conversely, sure, if the magician came out and said, 'Hey, you know what, I really did saw Betty in half – want to see her torso do back flips while her lower half sits on your lap?' you'd be impressed. You'd throw up but you'd be impressed. However, this isn't going to happen.

They start off with a kit when they're about seven, and spend Christmas Day boring the pants off relatives . . .

All this, by the way, relates to live magic. The sort where you know they're at least doing the trick properly. You know they're sweating a bit in that vampire waiter outfit. You know there's a couple of crushed doves under that cape, and a chance that the string of flags has got caught in the conjurer's underwear. And if not, there's a very real possibility that, when El Magico says to whichever crowned head of Europe who's in the royal box that evening, 'And was your card the three of hearts?' the crowned head is going to say, 'No, it was the nine of diamonds, you're crap.'

CLOWNS (1)
∿

Don't even go there.

JUGGLERS
∿

It's not a real skill. It's just catching multiplied. And why do they always have to look up when they're doing it? It's like typists who have to look at the keyboard when they type. Jugglers should be made to do it blindfold. With grenades.

MIME ARTISTS
∿

They all have stupid white-face make-up like some sort of bizarre reversal of the black and white minstrels, possibly from a world where the slaves won the American Civil War and decided to mock Whitey. They all wear body-stockings, which is both disturbing and unpleasant. And what's with the Breton shirts? Do they all hope to secretly be mistaken for French fishermen? Because it won't work; they'll still be thrown into the sea with the rest of the street 'entertainers'.

The same goes for those silver-painted human statues, except for one thing: on what planet are statues silver? Bronze, yes, concrete, marble, yeah, but silver? Is that so kids can go, 'He's not a real statue,' and kick him in the nuts?

PIZZA-DELIVERY 'BOYS'

∼

Maybe the phrase 'pizza face' is what inspires so many young men with appalling acne to become pizza delivery boys. It's nothing to do with adolescence, either, as most of these 'boys' are strapping great Turkish men in their early thirties. Maybe there's a big advert in the job centre that says:

WANTED
PEOPLE WITH BAD SKIN TO DELIVER FOOD
THAT RESEMBLES BAD SKIN

No-one really knows, but for some reason all pizza-delivery boys have spots like a Braille leopard. This we should not hold against them; especially when there are so many other things we can hold against them instead. Like never having change. All these boys do is deliver pizzas and take money off people. Yet offer them a ten-pound note for a nine-pound-forty order and it's as if you'd asked them to take over the government of a small European monarchy. In fact, they'd react better to the words, 'Egad, Mountvon! This lad has a look of Prince Rupert of Nancystein!' than 'Have you got change of a ten pound note?'

Then there's sense of direction. A pizza-delivery boy can get lost within a quarter of a kilometre of his place of work. He can get lost in the same street. If you want to see him implode, order a pizza and ask it to be delivered to the pizza parlour. This will set up a neural loop and he will go bang.

And how about time? Time is, we know now from Einstein and that, a relative concept. This was once a controversial theory. If they'd had pizza-delivery boys in Einstein's day, it wouldn't have been a controversial theory at all. It would have been a shoe-in. All Professor Einstein would have had to do to prove that time is relative would be order a couple of pizzas. The pizza parlour would tell him, 'Ten minutes,' and, sure enough, eight hours later, the pizzas would arrive. And, to prove the theory, they'd still be hot.

CLOWNS (2)
∾

All right. Where do we begin with clowns?

1) They're not funny. Ever. Which is a bit of a hindrance if being funny is your sole reason for existence.

2) They're frightening.

3) They're really not funny. Has anyone ever in the world ever laughed at that flower-squirting-water thing? Apart from, maybe, Hitler.

4) They're really frightening. If a bunch of horror writers sat down and said, 'Hey! Let's try and invent a figure which embodies all the elements of terror and fear there are,' they'd probably come up with a clown. A huge shock of electrocuted hair, deathly

white face-paint, garish voodoo make-up, a freakish costume and the laughter of the damned? It's a clown.

5) *Send In The Clowns*. Which always sounded not so much like a romantic ballad of loss and regret as a threat.

6) They're really, really, really not funny. Clown humour is based entirely on falling over whenever you hear a bass drum, riding round for what feels like hours in a car with an elliptical wheel, and having a dog in a pierrot costume run about barking. Again, all these are better suited to the novels of Stephen King than the world of family entertainment.

7) Jerry Lewis, the freakishly unamusing pretend epileptic, once made a film called *The Day The Clown Cried*, about a clown in the Nazi death camps. This film was deemed so mawkish that the movie company refused to release it. Yet, unlike as with other legendary lost or banned movies – *A Clockwork Orange*, the unedited *Wicker Man*, Abel Ganz's *Napoleon* – no-one has ever clamoured for this film to be released. Why? Because it's about a clown.

8) The only clown fact that anyone can remember is that each clown's make-up is unique. Yeah, uniquely crap. And how many variations on bad lipstick and a stupid cross on each eye can there be? How many different kinds of ginger fright wig are there?

9) They work in circuses.

10) They have stupid, unfunny names. Coco. Bozo. Booboo. Numnum. Unfunnio The Clown.

11) Famous clown fans include the serial killer John Wayne Gacey and the children's entertainer Michael Jackson.

12) Everyone talks about clowns who are crying on the inside. Like that's a bad thing.

13) On a happier note, in the USA a couple of years ago, 17 student clowns (yes) went to a shopping mall to do some clowning in front of shoppers, and were immediately asked to leave by a security guard. Proof, if proof be needed, that no-one likes clowns, not even harrassed, unhappy security guards, who you'd think would welcome the break.

14) Clown schools. As if it's not enough for ageing alcoholics who failed their Santa Claus test to take up clowning for a living, we now have the children of the middle classes going to clown schools, where, presumably, they learn such subjects as Draining The Humour Out Of Everyday Situations, Falling Down Is Hilarious! and Fires – A Rich Source Of Merriment.

15) They have been a bad influence on rock music. Any band whose members dress like clowns, wear 'sinister' clown masks, or name themselves after clowns, is going to be rubbish. Woo! We're scary clowns! Run away! Don't think so.

16) Their own claim to respectability is that their origins lie in the commedia del'arte of the Italian Renaissance or some such nonsense. So what? That's where we get pantomime from, and that's not respectable, it's just an onstage drying-out clinic for failed soap stars.

17) Pierrots. The Waffen SS of clowns. They're not even meant to be funny.

18) And, by extension, pierrot dolls.

19) They have done nothing for art. There are no great statues of clowns. Every great artist from Titian to Constable has avoided clowns. The only representations of clowns in painting are those crap paintings of green clowns crying that you find in car boot sales in remote rural areas.

20) Ronald McDonald.

BUSKERS

All buskers believe that The Man is stopping them becoming rich and famous, and if only the people could hear their fantastic music, they would be massive. The fact that The Man keeps doing them favours, like inventing Busking Areas and not having a special Busking Death Patrol that blows the head off any divot with a guitar and a harmonica holder does not occur to them in their vile arrogance.

Buskers do not so much add to the sum of human happiness as subtract from the sum of human happiness and then divide it by a million. They have a variety of unique busker skills, all of which can be learned by any fool in a few minutes. And they have their own code.

THE BUSKER'S CODE

i. I promise to never play anything original, interesting or fresh. The repertoire of Bob Dylan, Bob Marley and The Beatles will be the rock upon which I shall build my boring repertoire, with special reference to Blowing In The Wind, One Love, *and bloody* Yesterday.

ii. I will occasionally feature my own compositions. These will closely resemble the work of Bob Dylan, Bob Marley and The Beatles, except there will be a yodelling section near the end.

iii. If I am a classical busker, I shall restrict my repertoire to the most popular seasons out of The Four Seasons.

iv. If I am a jazz busker, I shall only play the saxophone, and my selections will consist of the following: Time After Time *by Cyndi Lauper, and the saxophone bit from* Will You *by Hazel O'Connor.*

v. I shall spurn all artificial instrumentation and modern fakery. I will however permit myself the use of a crap drum machine along with which I will find it impossible to keep time. And an amplifier.

vi. *If I am an acoustic guitarist, I must have a harmonica, on a stupid holder, so that in theory I can play the guitar and blow my harp at the same time. In practice this is a bit hard, so I don't actually do it. But I could.*

---

vii. *If I am an electric guitarist, I will have not only an amplifier and a drum machine but also I will not sing out of tune versions of pop songs. I will play out of tune pop instrumentals that start out sounding familiar and then meander off into pointless soloing as though my guitar had got Alzheimer's.*

---

viii. *Style. I will wear old jeans, a black waistcoat and a sort of green shirt with different fabrics sewn on it. If I am a jazz musician, I will wear a stupid trilby and sunglasses. I may also wear a red bandanna, but only on condition that, should I have a dog, the dog will also wear a red bandanna.*

---

ix. *Manners. If someone walks by and throws money into my hat, I will ignore them as I am concentrating on my art. If however, someone walks by and doesn't throw money into my hat, I will mutter something ungracious.*

---

x. *The law. The Man is out to get me and stamp down on my original, inventive, futuristic music. I do not however support the legalisation of busking as then everyone will be doing it and I will be forced to get a job in an arts centre serving carrot cake with a surly expression.*

THE YOUNG

*'Teenagers should be shot into space
until they reach their mid-20s.'*

BABIES

~

Like a Stuka screaming in to deliver a bombload of steaming poop,
babies are the mewling, puking, crapping schocktroops of the
pre-nursery generation. Are they mad? They look mad. They spend
an awful lot of time pointing at nothing. What do they want? They
eat appalling food. They make no sense. They make a noise with one
end that sounds worse than foxes having it off and they make a smell
at the other that stinks like the town dump is outside on the lawn
knocking on the front door.

They are more self-obssessed than a supermodel on angel dust and
they could interrupt the sleep of the dead. In fact, forget all those
defibrilation paddles and massive injections of adrenalin, any time a
surgeon wants to bring a comatose or dead person round, all he
needs to do is hold a screaming, self-cacking baby over the operating
table. They have terrible taste in clothes. They even have special furniture. You can't play with their toys, which are weird and boring.
They don't do any work, and they haven't any money. And their only
ambition seems to be to make appalling smells. Worse, later on they
become teenagers (see TEENAGERS). What were they thinking?

SCHOOLCHILDREN

~

Schoolchildren are like normal children only psychotic. They are
armed, dangerous, violent, rude, unkempt and obsessed with

smoking behind bike sheds (the rate of juvenile bronchitis in Holland, land of bicycles, must be through the roof). There can be no displeasure greater than that of getting on a bus and discovering it is full of schoolkids on their way home. Hear the level of wit sink to the earth's core. Observe first-hand violence at its rawest. Listen as young middle class kiddies from Esher affect, with little competence, the dialects of gangsta rappers and 'Yardies'. Blush at sexually explicit language that would cause a pimp to curl up and die. And that, as they used to say on the halls, is just the girls... .

TEENAGERS

Everything bad about children meets everything bad about adults in one spot-faced, surly, shuffling tit. Parents spend years of their lives and thousands of their pounds raising these acne cuckoos. They cover them in love, worry themselves sick about them, go out of their way to make sacrifices for them and ensure that the little freaks enjoy a decent childhood. And their reward is this: ingratitude in barely human form. Resentful festering grudges in PORN STAR t-shirts (see PEOPLE WHO WEAR 'PORN STAR' T-SHIRTS). They should be shot into space until they reach their mid-20s. Here are some things you may well find yourself wanting to say to a teenager.

1) 'Stand up straight, do you want to be a hunchback?'

2) 'What? What did you say? Stop mumbling.'

3) 'Where are you going with that skateboard? You can barely walk, let alone operate a piece of wood on rollerskate wheels.'

4) 'What are you smoking? Oh good, now you're even less articulate, mobile and interesting than you were ten minutes ago. Here, have some heroin, it's more debilitating.'

5) 'Yes, you can have a car on your 16th birthday. Would you like a Rolls Royce? Or perhaps a humvee. After all, you've done sod all in the past 15 years to earn it. Here, have my cashpoint card.'

6) 'No, you can't sleep with your girlfriend. Why not? Well a) you haven't got one, because phoning someone up and ringing off

isn't a relationship b) if you did have one, the pleasure of having sex in your room with the Noddy wallpaper painted black and the crunch of PlayStation remote controls under foot would be slender and c) given you still secretly think that you can get pregnant through kissing with tongues, you may not be ready for the full on majesty of sexual union.'

7) 'It's not fair? No, fair would be me kicking you downstairs and into an Army Recruiting Office.'

8) 'I'm not too old to appreciate your record collection, you just seem to have the worst taste in music since Hitler. If these bands really want to offend society, maybe they should try sacking their stylist first. Keeping it real? They make The Monkees look completely authentic.'

9) 'Yes, fart gags are funny. And guaranteed to make top models have sex with you. When you make that farting noise and fall over laughing, it's like Oscar Wilde has rejoined us from the grave.'

10) 'You wish you'd never been born? You weren't, we made you out of spare body parts and rejected pig organs. You've only got a week to live, in fact, and then we're going to eat you.'

STUDENTS

Students used to at least be interesting. In the old days, they all wore jazz beards, smoked jazz fags and listened to folk music. They went on CND marches and drank real ale. They were a bit heavy-going socially, but at least they were never going to nick your girlfriend and later on some of them would invent Monty Python, which isn't a bad thing really. Then they found better drugs, grew their hair, started dressing like members of the Grateful Dead and got weird. They abandoned jazz and CND for heavy rock and sit-ins, knew how to spell 'Kierkegaard' and said 'Man' a bit too often. They were now more likely to nick your girlfriend, but at least they were a bit more fun socially and later on some of them would invent the internet, or computers or Virgin (see VIRGIN TRAINS).

And then Margaret Thatcher got in. Having neutralised the unions, the Labour Party and Ben Elton, Thatcher realised that her only remaining opposition was students, so she took away their grants and made sure they'd never be able to pay their own way unless they all got jobs when they left college. Now students are annoying in a different way. This lot can no longer be found dismantling road furniture at three in the morning or bringing the London rush-hour to a standstill because they are all far too busy swatting up on business management and planning how to rid themselves of 13 grand's worth of debt. Loads of eager specky gits in Bhs suits desperate to learn how to make as much money as possible and become head of ICI before Christmas. People barely out of their teens who should be lying in a pool of cider somewhere are instead getting drunk on the concept of middle management. Intellects who once would have devoted their lives to becoming quite good at Asteroids are now struggling to master the organisational infrastructure of Asda.

None of this would be so bad, were it not for the fact that students a) eventually leave college and make all the telly and the books and magazines that we read and b) go on drug-addled gap years and accidentally invent the internet, or computers or ways of illegally downloading music. With the lot we're currently turning out, the future is going to be one long sales conference stamping on a human face for ever.

> People barely out of their teens who should be lying in a pool of cider somewhere are instead getting drunk on the concept of middle management.

PUBLIC HOLIDAYS

'The way things are headed we'll all be out on Christmas Day because we've got to get started on next year's Christmas shopping.'

CHRISTMAS
〜

1) Here's a clue. December the 25th. Not September the 25th, or June the 25th or May the 8th. December the 25th. Christmas starts earlier every year. The way things are headed we'll all be out on Christmas Day because we've got to get started on next year's Christmas shopping.

2) Christmas cards. All greetings cards are bad (see GREETINGS CARDS), but Christmas cards are particularly egregious. Since when did we have to start sending Christmas cards to everyone we've ever met? Family, yes, close friends, sure, people we're having sex with, fine, but after that, it all gets a bit tenuous. A couple we met on holiday? If we have to. The postman? Like he wants to see another Christmas card. The woman who lived next door to us ten years ago but we moved? Pushing it there. Queen Beatrix of the Netherlands? She's never sent us one. And so it goes, until one day you are spending £45,000 a year on stamps to send festive greetings to a lot of complete strangers. Worst of all, even though they don't know who you are, out of politeness they send a card too, and you have a house full of Christmas cards. Whole forests are dying for this nonsense.

3) People who, at this time of year, say, 'Ooh, it's so commercial nowadays.' There are two things here:
• When was the last time Christmas wasn't commercial? 1406? No-one's that old.

• Why are these people complaining? Are they deeply religious? Unlikely.

> 'Ooh, Christmas is so commercial nowadays.'
>> *'I'll be seeing you in church this Sunday, then. What? You don't go to church?'*
> 'No, we – '
>> *'I see. So, given that the religious aspect of Christmas is meaningless for you and that you despise the commercial aspects, presumably not only do you not go to church, but also you don't buy any presents. Oh! You do buy presents. Well, SHUT UP THEN.'*

4) For the rest of us, who don't carp on about commercialism because if we keep our gobs shut we might get some nice stuff, the real vexation of Christmas is the fact that we have to fork out billions of pounds for presents, despite knowing full well that what we are buying will be half price in the sales only a few days later. See, when it's a SALE ITEM, it's a bit of bargain tat. But when it's a PRESENT, it's a barely unattainable object of desire. Life's funny that way.

5) Relatives. They say you can choose your friends but not your relatives. That is true, but most of the time you can at least choose which relatives you're going to see. Cousin Alec with the odd smell and Auntie Mary whose stories revolve around operations and funerals are not on that list. Come Christmas, however, and they're on you like a vampire. Relatives live for Christmas; it's the only time they're allowed inside other people's houses for any length of time. Bang, they're in the good armchair. Whoosh, they've got the remote and they're in charge of the telly. Glug, and there goes your nice single malt. At any other time of the year, they'd just be burglars but at Christmas, you have to be nice to them.

6) Children. Like relatives only more dangerous. Children are the ones about whom Christmas is often supposed to be all about. They acknowledge their place in the festive scheme by becoming obsessed with the Nativity, an event that until mid-November was unknown

to them. This is solely so they can get a part as a Wise Man or an Angel or a Sheep in a play so bad that even Japanese tourists wouldn't go. And then they want presents. Children make the last Roman emperors look altruistic. The way they choose gifts is to look at the price and pick the item that costs the most. If they don't get it, they will cry and fight. If they do get it, they will unwrap it in a flurry of excitement, play with it for ten seconds, and then never look at it again. Then they will get fractious. As you are unable to sedate them with sherry, children will get more sullen and ratty as the day goes

on, start crying during the Disney film and later vomit a lot. In later years they will look back on all this crying and vomiting and fixation on material goods as 'the happiest time of my life'.

7) The lights. There's something about Christmas lights. Once upon a time they seemed special. Of course, the lens of nostalgia might explain this, but the fact is that nowadays they are, well, manky. Now this might be acceptable in, say, a fishing village or a slum, but not in the major shopping thoroughfares of the land. It's one thing for a

crack-addled housing estate to not be able to put up anything more than a few crusty snowmen and wonky reindeer, but you expect a bit more from Oxford Street, Princes Street and other major trading streets. All that fuss, Charlotte Church down to turn them on, and what do you get? Some neon tat that wouldn't look out of place in a

All that fuss, Charlotte Church down to turn them on, and what do you get? Some neon tat that wouldn't look out of place in a stripclub in 1930s Las Vegas.

stripclub in 1930s Las Vegas. These rotten lights are paid for, by the way, by some of the most profitable stores and businesses in the world, the skinflint bastards. Which means not only do we have to look at some sort of vile widdle-coloured winking Santa that appears to have been designed by a one-eyed cat, but also it's got the logo of a fizzy drinks manufacturer stuck on it.

8) Telly:

a) *Christmas Movies*. The, if you will, diptych of Christmas movies on the telly is two films in particular, *The Sound Of Music* and *The Great Escape*, which both feature dramatic chases involving Nazis. That tells you a lot about the British notion of Christmas. War, nuns and prison camps. Sometimes we might get *The Battle Of Britain* instead. What we will also definitely get is a James Bond film. Nothing wrong with that but again, why do programme planners associate Christmas with shagging and international espionage? There's none of that in the New Testament.

b) *Repeats*. There is no denying that Morecambe and Wise were great.

Their TV shows stand up well, even today, a third of a century later. The scripts, comic timing, repartee and guests were of the highest standard. However, there cannot be a child in the land who has not seen every single one of the Morecambe and Wise Christmas specials. And while Morecambe and Wise are deservedly recognisable to millions, it has to be said that some of their guests are not. Even despite the popularity of nostalgia shows, most viewers would be hard-pressed to name all the former celebs in the skit with the dancing sailors. This is because virtually every single one of the sailors apart from Parky is dead. Why don't they either dig out some shows that Morecambe and Wise made which weren't Christmas specials? Or even make some new sodding TV shows?

The same goes for *The Two Ronnies*. And *Some Mothers Do 'Ave 'Em*, with bells on.

c) *Sitcom specials*:

'I really used to like that sitcom. You know, it was big in the '90s.'

'Well, you're in luck. They're doing a Christmas one-off.'

'Really? But it hasn't been on for 10 years. The cast must be pushing 60 by now.'

'They are, and they'd rather be in something new. But the writer's been persuaded to push the creaky old boat out one more time.'

'So what's the story?'

'There isn't one. But they do go to Miami.'

'That's not very original. They always go to Miami in these specials.'

'Yes, I think the TV company have a secret deal with some Cuban drug lords.'

'So a half hour of old-fashioned fun. I can handle that.'

'A half hour? Are you mad? Two hours. Spread out over the whole weekend.'

'Dear Lord. What's on the other side?'

'Remember that other sitcom that was big in the '90s? Same thing.'

9) Games. These days games are something kids play on their own, in their bedrooms, on computers. Games reflect the latest in technology and have levels of realism and complexity that were impossible barely half a decade ago. On Christmas Day, teenagers race to their rooms to simulate underground combat with zombies or road-racing contests in the 43rd century. Meanwhile, we're all in the front room, arguing about who's going to be the boot. It's not fair. Next year, give yourself the latest computer games and stay downstairs having techie fun, and send the kids to their rooms with a Bumper Fun Box of Snakes And Ladders.

10) The Queen's Speech. Once the Queen is no longer with us, it would be ace if we could get rid of this. It's fine when it's the Queen – it's like a very short visit from a slightly bizarre aunt who's got a thing about the Commonwealth – but her successors are a different kettle of chinless fish. If the blond kid becomes king, we're in for something which will be not so much a message to the nation as a Sloane's thank-you letter: 'Christmas was brill this year, Harry got a bike and I got Scotland.' And as for his dad – dear Lord, is there enough videotape in the world for that man's idea of a Xmas message? With his boring eco-warrior toff image he's like a cross between Bertie Wooster and Sting and his message would reflect that. Then again, if the BBC has got any sense, they'll just point a camera at him and not bother putting any film in it.

VALENTINE'S DAY

∼

Named, by the way, after Saint Valentine, so technically is called Saint Valentine's Day, but shortened in popular use to avoid offending the many saint-haters we hear so much about nowadays. The original Saint Valentine was a Roman priest who married people during time of war when it was illegal, and was executed for it by, of all people, the Emperor 'I' Claudius. Some cynics might suggest that, by way of compensation, there ought to be a Claudius' Day, where soft-headed romantics are executed for spending 200 quid on a red plush teddy bear, sending out vile syrupy chocolates, killing thousands of flowers just to say, 'I want sex', and so forth.

Valentine's Day is a romantic event, and as such, is part of the romance industry. When you send a Valentine's card, unsigned presumably so as to avoid breaching that exclusion order, you are working for The Romance Man.

BONFIRE NIGHT

∾

Takes place a month and 20 days before Christmas, not that you'd know. Kids start collecting money for weapons round about the same time Christmas cards start appearing in the shops. Like a tiny IRA, they rattle their buckets at people when summer's light begins to fade. Follow them all the way home and lob a grenade over their parents' wall.

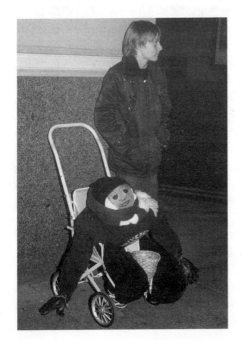

Kids start collecting money for weapons round about the same time Christmas cards start appearing in the shops.

Guy Fawkes Night has been spoiled by three things. Safety regulations, which are designed to make the fiery hell of Bonfire Night as tame and tiresome as possible. Secondly, kids, who think 'Bonfire Night' is French for 'all bloody year'. How the novelty palls when the little rascals are letting off giant rockets at the end of your street for three straight months. And then there's the extortion trail. Time was when the little ruffian scum at least used to have a Guy in a pram to show people; these days, the pram's been sold and their mum won't let them have the buggy, and they can't be arsed to make a Guy anyway. Why not cut out the middleman and put them on a bonfire? That way everyone's happy.

GREETINGS CARDS
❧

Birthdays, fine. Christmas, all right (but see CHRISTMAS). Mother's day, if we must. Get well soon, why not. But that's it. There is a greetings card for every event bar OPEN A WINDOW, I'VE JUST BROKEN WIND! There are cards for religious festivals that you have never celebrated, relations you've never met, and minor work occasions that ought to be kept quiet (WELL DONE, CREEPY! YOUR BUM-LICKING HAS GOT YOU PROMOTED TO ASSISTANT JUNIOR DEPUTY SOMETHING OR OTHER). There are 'humorous' cards, which are never funny, serious cards, which are often unintentionally funny, cards for boys and girls which seem to have been teleported in from 1958, unless racing cars are still cigar-shaped and bright green, musical ones which contain nothing that could be called music, sexy cards which would turn a pervert's stomach, and ironic cards which would make Noel Coward wish he'd never invented irony.

All this wouldn't be so bad (well, it would, but let's try and see some sunlight here) if the bloody things didn't cost so much. It's a piece of cardboard, folded in the middle, with a stupid picture on the front and a stupid message on the inside. How much can it cost to make? A penny? Three pence? Four? And how much does it 'retail' for? Three pounds and 99 pence. How the hell did greetings cards manufacturers manage to do that? It's not like there's a tax on them – although there ought to be: *'The Chancellor today announced nine pence on beer, seven pence on cigarettes and an extra four pounds 50 tax on greetings cards'.*

To save money, either make your own, don't send any at all, or wait till three or four events in someone's life come along at once and send them a unicard:

Congratulations on your promotion
At this sad time in your life

•

Happy Birthday
And get well soon
This Diwali!

PEOPLE WHO...

*'People with no manners
should be put in a big grinder and minced.'*

... USE A TRAIN CARRIAGE LIKE IT'S THEIR OFFICE

~

There you are, enduring a train journey, crammed in next to a backpacker and a man who is taking his lager collection on holiday, when the voice starts. 'Hello, Carol, I'm on the train,' it begins innocuously. And then it goes on, and on, and on. 'Can you chase up that invoice?' 'I need the document on my desk asap.' Asap isn't a word. 'I think we should use a different supplier.' How about a heroin supplier? That might shut you up. Then marvellous silence. Then, 'Sorry, we went into a tunnel.' Shame it wasn't a black hole. 'Listen, did Jerry call?' No, Jerry actually has some work to do. Can none of this waffling gob toss be done when you get into work? What the hell do you talk to Carol about when you arrive at the office?

There are ways of dealing with this fool. Sadly, removing his head with one clean swing of a baseball bat is illegal. The best thing to do is sit opposite him, turn on your mobile phone and say, 'Hi, Carol, yes, I'm on the train with him now. Yes, he's talking like his tongue has declared independence from his brain. Yes, he's banging on about using a different supplier. No, he's still got that cheap suit. No, he's talking so loudly he couldn't hear me if I put my mouth to his ear and screamed into it. Yes, he has noticed me now. Yes, he looks vaguely upset. Yes, other people are laughing now. Yes, he's gone into the loo. Yes, I'm following him. Yes, he looks vaguely upset. Yes, I'm stroking the nape of his neck. No, he doesn't like it... .'

Works every time.

... THROW THINGS OUT OF THE CAR WINDOW
⌒

The motorway is your dustbin. And so is your brain. Look, we've seen your car. It smells like a turd's armpit already so why not keep your rubbish in it. All of your rubbish, like your skinny wife and your fat kids. And you. Hey, save us all time, drive down the scrap-yard and put yourself in the crusher. You'll not be missed.

... HAVEN'T BOUGHT A WEEKEND SAVER
⌒

These people are always tutters. They are the kind of monkeys' bums who 'always buy a first class ticket, it's so much more comfortable and the cost is negligible when you set it next to the convenience'. What they mean by this is simply, 'I hate poor people.'

The only way to deal with these idiots is to travel with one of the rail companies that still does weekend savers, obviously on an occasion when the savers are in force, say for example a weekend. Before doing so, dress in the manner of a tramp who is so tatty that other tramps call him 'Trampy', buy a big bucket of fake KFC Chicken (the kind named after an American state not famous for fried chicken, like say Oregon) and a copy of *The Sun*. Then sit opposite someone who looks like they bought a proper first class ticket. They are pretty easy to spot, as they tend to dress like they are going to an audition for *All Creatures Great And Small*, i.e. they're wearing a tweed jacket with leather elbow patches or gold-rimmmed glasses for looking over. Open your newspaper, start eating a chili chicken leg, and if they tut, you've got 'em.

... PREFER ANIMALS TO HUMAN BEINGS
⌒

'I'm just not comfortable with people,' they say. What they mean is, 'I'm a complete freak who nobody wants to talk to, so I've bought a budgerigar.' Weirdoes. There's nothing wrong with having a pet, or liking animals or even keeping a zebra if you have to, but where we get the bus to Freakytown is when people start making a thing of it. So you've got five cats? A) big deal. B) Get one more cat and you officially qualify as a nutter.

The worst thing about animal lovers (apart from the smell) is their insistence that animals are somehow superior to people. If they are then how come they haven't got us building the pyramids (see CATS) and also you just want to say, 'why don't you become one then'? People who aren't comfortable with the gender they were born into are perfectly happy to go under the knife and have a sex change; why don't these animal fans go one better and have a species change? It would be a sensible use of gene technology and lots funnier than sticking an ear on a mouse. Imagine Mrs Thompson from the wool shop walking down the street having been done up into a dog and really wanting a wee. Oh, the clash of value systems.

And another thing. Should there not be some kind of law to stop these people leaving all their money to a sodding cats' home? Here's a cat – he's nocturnal, he lives on mice, birds and things he finds in the dustbin. He's asleep on the fence all day long and shagging other cats most of the night. What does he really need most of all in the world? A gun? An endless supply of catfood? A new ear? Yes to all of these. What does he really, really not need? That's right; a house. A cat does not need a house. For a start, there's the mortgage. And if the will doesn't cover the council tax, who's going to mow the lawn? Not Mister Tibbles, that's for sure.

... HAVE TOO MUCH LUGGAGE

'Excuse me, my flight leaves in ten minutes, I've only got hand baggage, could I be a pain and check-in in front of you?'

'No, I'm sorry, we have 25 pieces of luggage, all matching and we need to take all frigging day to check it in.'

'But I'm only –'

'First of all we're going to have a laugh and try and get it all on as hand-baggage. Then we'll get shirty and wave our arms around a lot. And then after a bit we'll give in and let them put it in the hold.'

'I just –'

'I know what you're thinking. Why do we have all these pieces of luggage when we're only going to see Aunt Louisa in Boulogne? That's a good question. I think the answer is we don't care what's in the cases. The fact is, we collect luggage the way other people collect stamps. And one day we hope to own every single piece of luggage in the world.'

... ARE OBSSESSED WITH THEIR COUNTRY
~

Your country is very nice. We'd all like to go there on holiday. Your economy is either better than ours or worse than ours; either way, it's meaningless. Goodness me, what a lot of wars your country has been in. Gosh, it really has been around for a very long time. Well done. Now bugger off. It's just another country, the

Goodness me, what a lot of wars your country has been in. Gosh, it really has been around for a very long time. Well done. Now bugger off.

world's full of them. Here, have this globe; blimey, look at all those countries! No, the blue bit isn't a very big country, it's the sea. Take your flag down off your window or your flagpole, teach your kids your weird language but don't make anyone else speak it, support your sporting team quietly and without waving your arms, crying or hitting anyone who doesn't support your sporting team, and shut up.

And that goes for all the tossers who think that we should all have a holiday on Saint George's Day when most of them are too arse-holed on either single malt or super-strength lager to go to work in the first place.

... FIND ACCIDENTS FASCINATING
~

Whenever two or three are gathered, you can be sure that they are watching some poor sod who's been in an accident. These days we can't actually throw Jehovah's Witnesses to the lions, alas, or burn Scientologists for witches, but we can get our sicko jollies watching people trapped in burning wreckage or thrown from their motorbikes. And then a policeman comes along and says, 'Move along, nothing to see.' This is a lie. If he was breaking up a crowd of people outside a TV shop watching something on Channel Five and said 'Move along, nothing to see,' fair enough.

But the whole point of accidents as entertainment is that there is something to see. The police should cordon off the area and charge people to look at the accident if they want. That would separate the men from the ghouls.

... THINK THEY HAVE 'STREET CRED' (1)

∾

What are you talking about? Why are you superior because you talk in glottal stops? Just because you go round telling people that you were born in a skip and raised by litter doesn't mean that you're better than anyone else.

Inverted snobbery they call it, although 'being an arsehole' is an equally good phrase. Once upon a time you were only a good person if you were a duke or similar. Now we don't have feudalism, we have 'cool', and status is reckoned by how 'street' someone is. Have you seen any streets lately? They're full of burst bin bags and tramp waz. Not much of a role model. 'Hi, I've based my whole life on Trumpington Villas.' 'Wow, that's so credible.'

Street credulous, more like.

... THINK THEY HAVE 'STREET CRED' (2)

∾

And don't think for one moment that anyone really believes you were born in a skip and raised by litter. Bend an ear for a second to those carefully mangled vowels and anyone can tell that the only estate you've ever been near was a country estate.

The last time anyone was responsible for a teenage pregnancy in your family, it was your great-great-great uncle, who got a parlour-maid up the duff. So take off those ridiculous baggy trousers, do your shoe laces up, and go and get a job in the city before some people who really did grow up on a council estate tip you head-first into some bins. Matey.

... PUT PICTURES OF THEIR FAMILY ON THEIR CHRISTMAS CARDS
◇

Oh here's a festive scene. Alice and Ian Thompson, with their dog. Wow. What a lovely image. Because obviously when we think of Christmas, we think of the Thompson family. Never mind Santa Claus and robins and the birth of Jesus, Christmas is all about Alice and Ian Thompson and their dog. I just can't wait to see their Easter card.

... PARK IN DISABLED SPACES WHEN NOT ENTITLED
◇

You're not disabled. But that could be arranged.

... COLLECT TOYS
◇

Those baby boomer sad cases, who are so reluctant to let go of their pre-teenage years that they keep on buying Dinky Toys and Action Men and (in some cases) Barbies. There are children, in orphanages and war zones, who would love to have a decent toy, but they can't because, instead of giving their toys to Oxfam, these sad overgrown nappy-wearers are keeping them all. 'That's a nice dolly.' 'I'm sorry, Sergei, it's a vintage Air Hostess Sindy and it's worth £2000.'

Most annoying of all are the tossers who collect the Star Wars 'fig-urines' or toys, as we used to call them. Which they keep in the orig-inal bubble wrap. This is appalling. If you're going to be a grown man who collects little toy space soldiers, the least you can do is get them out the packaging and march them around the room, making little 'pee-oo' noises to represent gunfire. Oh, go to hell.

... LITTER
◇

Oi! Worthless cacking human scum. Pick that up, before some-one forces it down your perpetually open throat. The planet is

Possibly your brain can only cope with
the instructions 'Purchase McDonald's,'
'Eat McDonald's,' and 'Throw McDonald's
wrapper onto the pavement.'

sinking under the sheer tonnage of human waste and your solution is to add to it. Possibly you don't care that the Earth is now so weighed down with crap that it will probably sink into the sun fairly soon. Possibly your brain can only cope with the instructions 'Purchase McDonald's,' 'Eat McDonald's,' and 'Throw McDonald's wrapper onto the pavement.'

Hey posh retard! Maybe you value your luxury townhouse so much that actually waiting till you get home to unwrap your purchases and not filling the streets with cellophane and cardboard is not an option.

Good morning, van driver! Why not leave that coke can and fag packet in the van with the rest of the stinking snack filth you have made a fat driver's nest in.

Hello former washing machine owner! How about calling the council to have that taken away, rather than waiting for the washing machine fairy? In fact, why not call the sodding council and have them take you away.

At least litter has an excuse for acting like garbage.

... PLAY POKER

It's a card game, you gits. Just because you sit around a baize table and wear silly visors like old ladies at the beach and smoke cigars and drink big men's whisky drinks doesn't make it any different to three card brag or whist like your granny used to play. Speaking of whom, your granny could beat the lot of you blindfold.

Poker is just snap for people who want to play at being grown-ups. All the stupid names like 'three card stud' and 'donkey bluff' or whatever are just dressing up. And as for 'professional' poker players? Get a job, Happy Families boy.

... LET THEIR CHILDREN RECORD MESSAGES ON THEIR ANSWERING MACHINE

'Hello, mummy and daddy can't come to the phone right now. Please leave a muh... a message'. What, are you too idle to record your own message? Are you so drunk by teatime that you have to get the kids to do it instead? Or – as presumably is the case – do you think your kids are so fantastic that you want everyone who rings up to know?

Why don't you go the whole hog? Get the kids to drive you to work. Have them do your accounts. Or maybe take your place at an important conference. You might as well, your answering machine message has just told the whole world that you have alphabetti spaghetti instead of a brain.

... SEND 'ROUND ROBIN' LETTERS
~

'Merry Xmas. Well, it's been quite a year in the Jennings household, I can tell you! Phil got promoted at his job in *PLACE YOU'VE NEVER HEARD OF AND COULDN'T GIVE A FIG ABOUT EVEN IF IT CAME ROUND AND BIT YOU* and now he's in charge of *SOMETHING SO BORING THAT THINKING ABOUT IT MIGHT KILL YOU.* The children are fine, and we are delighted because *SOME KID YOU HAVE NEVER MET* has passed some exam or other/ learned a simple task/ been released from borstal.

This year we went on holiday in *PLACE YOU HAVE NEVER HEARD OF BUT BET IT'S REALLY EXPENSIVE.* Oh – nearly forgot! *OLD FRIEND OF THEIRS THAT YOU DON'T KNOW BUT THEY THINK YOU DO ALTHOUGH IN FACT IT'S HER FRIEND FROM COLLEGE WHO YOU HAVE NEVER MET* came by and said hello! He's married now – and guess who to! It's *SOME OTHER DIMWIT YOU'VE NEVER HEARD OF AND HOPE NEVER TO MEET.*

Well, got to close now – we're going round to *YOU DON'T KNOW WHO THE HELL THEY ARE EITHER* for dinner!'

... DRIVE WITH 'P' PLATES
❧

Learner drivers are one thing – we all have to learn to drive at some time in our lives. But when we have passed our driving test, surely the greatest pleasure of all – apart from not ever having to sit in a minicab (see MINICABS) again – is the moment when we throw away our L plates. That's literally throw away our L plates, by the way – send them spinning like rectangular frisbees into the bin or canal, whichever is nearer. It's a ritual moment acknowledged in all driving cultures.

But there is a new movement afoot, one where people throw away their L plates – and then get another set. P plates is what we're talking about here. The learner driver equivalent of keeping your stablisers on after you've learned to ride your bicycle. P plates, probably, are meant to tell the world, 'Hey world! Steady on, would you? I've just learned to drive and I'm kinda finding my feet, driving-wise.' This, sadly, is not the message that these green plates send out. The message they send out is more, 'Hey! I've learned to drive, technically, but I kinda like the idea that people will treat me with kid gloves and let me screw up and generally annoy the crap out of everyone else on the road.'

P. For prat.

... OWN PERSONALISED NUMBER PLATES
❧

Why do some people feel the need to personalise their cars? You wouldn't personalise your kids – put furry dice round their necks and go-faster stripes up their backs. You wouldn't remove their original noses and replace them with chrome-plated noses. And you certainly wouldn't spend 15 grand having your name written on them in the wrong lettering.

Personalised number plates don't even make sense. Some halfwit called Steven with a faint understanding of how to form letters will get a number plate like this: 5TE V3N. Now that may be good enough for him, and it might even have been a pretty good go at

writing STEVEN if it was, say, 1453 and we were still struggling towards some vaguely unified form of spelling, but in the 21st century, the only way that 5TE V3N is going to be the same word as STEVEN is if a lot of squinting is going to be allowed.

Actually, the real number plates that people have are bad enough. What child has not cried at the sheer numbing boredom of knowing that Paul Daniels' number plate is MAG 1C? Similarly, how come Jimmy Tarbuck has never fallen foul of the Advertising Standards Authority for his COM 1C plate. TOX 1C might be better. Or SH 1T.

... HAVE TATTOOS
∿

Hey! If you're going to get something that will last your entire life, try and get, say, some diamonds, or a castle, or a million pounds. Not a drawing that stretches with age. Or – worst of all – 'Celtic' tattoos. These look like bits of burning newspaper and are tattooed around the bulgy bicep like so many bitemarks. They are meant to indicate that you have a spiritual side, but really signify that the person who tattooed you had run out of coloured ink, pictures of anchors, and any good ideas. Celtic tattoos probably look great on some woad-covered warrior, running broadsworded-up to lop the head off some Roman. They look rubbish on a junior IT consultant from Tring.

... HAVE GOATEE BEARDS
∿

Should really be spelt 'goaty'. Makes you look like a hairy stamp got stuck on your chin. Either that or Hitler's lip reflection. Is meant to suggest an artistic temperament. Instead suggests you don't own a shaving mirror.

... GROW DESIGNER STUBBLE
∿

What designer is this? Mr Trampy?

... WEAR BOW TIES
∿

Are you a gay professor? Then take it off.

... WEAR TOPS THAT SHOW THEIR STOMACHS
∿

Why are all these people throwing up? Nothing to do with that huge wobbling tyre of ladygut, is it?

... WEAR 'PORN STAR' T-SHIRTS
∿

Do you suppose that actual real-life porn stars in Los Angeles go round wearing t-shirts that say 'SPOTTY VIRGIN FROM DORKING' or 'BANK CLERK WHO GETS DRUNK AFTER THREE GLASSES OF SPARKLING WHITE WINE?' No? Then why are you wearing a PORN STAR t-shirt, spotty virgin or bank clerk?

... TIE THEIR HAIR IN A PONY TAIL
∿

Only ever worn by men 'of a certain age' (i.e. over 40) who are going bald. The effect is supposed to be one of virility. Look at me! I may be over 40 but I can grow a thin stream of hair piss down the back of my neck! I've got a big one! The reality is sadder; with the big bald patch, a pony-tail makes the wearer look as though his hair is slipping slowly off the top of his head down his back.

... KEEP TALKING
∿

Shut up! Just shut up! Even if you don't understand the purpose of conversation you must have seen people in films occasionally NOT TALKING and leaving gaps for other people TO SPEAK IN. Why do you think you're interesting? Who cares if the dull piece of death-advancing language waste you're currently rolling out happened on a Wednesday or a Tuesday? It wouldn't be interesting if it happened in a wrinkle in time! SHUT UP! SHUT UP!

And if you can't shut up, try listening.

... DON'T LISTEN
∿

These wastes of lungs won't even stop when the very point of their gassing has been challenged.
'Have you ever been to York?'
   'Yes, I went last week.'
'Well, it's a very interesting place.'

'I know, I went last week.'

'There's one of Europe's oldest cathedrals there.'

'Yes, in fact that's why I went there. I was asked to become Archbishop of York.'

'In fact, it's a major ecclesiastical locus.'

'I'll major ecclesiastical locus you in a minute, you death-voiced fart-bladder! In fact, I am going to kill you! Yes! I could have been Archbishop of York but I threw it all away just to kill you! Die!'

'One of the most interesting things about Yoarghhh...uk'

Well, we can dream.

... DRINK ON THE PAVEMENT

~

Outside the pavement cafes of Paris and the terrazzas of Rome, street-drinking is a pleasant, relaxed affair. Outside a pub in Bolton, it's an act of madness. Are you ill, street-drinker? There's plenty of seats inside. Inside, where carbon monoxide doesn't mix with your fizzy lager. Inside, where furious passers-by don't have to shove past drunken would-be boulevardiers. It took mankind millions of years to invent being indoors, and two pints of piddle later you want to overthrow all *that*.

... SKATE ON THE PAVEMENT

~

Adults, too. It was almost OK when apple-cheeked lads with catapults used roller skates to get their ball back from old Mr van Morrison next door, but nowadays the real bumfaced thumbsuckers of the road are grown-ups. What's wrong with you, you arsehole? You're 35 years old and you've got a scooter. Do you still wet yourself as well? Are you still learning to read? A scooter? You know, you could learn to drive and everything. You can vote, although you'd probably cast your vote for Bagpuss, you childhood-obsessed cackmuncher. Roller blades? Aren't they just high heels for roller skaters? Get out of the way or we'll scythe your head off.

... HAVE NO MANNERS

〜

Manners are important. People with no manners should be put in a big grinder and minced. Here are a few tips:

1 Opening doors for men and women is nice, not letting them slam in someone's face like a giant rectangular wooden catapult.

2 Giving up your seat to older or more pregnant people is practical, as one day you might be one of them and would like to sit down, not receive the fatal battering with a length of scaffold pole that you actually deserve.

3 Driving as though you've noticed your car is a means to a destination not a demonstration of your sexuality is good too, especially as no-one over eight years old thinks that aggressively driving a cheap sports car is horny, just desperate. Oh, and if someone has gone out of their way to let you pass, just give them a little wave. It really does cost nothing – in fact, it's a little bit of exercise – it makes everyone feel better and it prevents anyone mistaking you for a pig-faced mannerless sack of goat guts.

4 Having good phone manners; when did people stop saying 'Bye!' in a cheerful, see-you-again kind of way, and start saying, 'Bye...' like a dying pig?

5 Thanking people. Again, a lost skill. If someone does you a favour or helps you, the correct response is not 'Good' or 'OK' it's 'Thank you for helping me, even though I am a mannerless fat toad who lives in a well of ignorance, ingratitude and bad breath.' That's always welcome.

6 Standing around when you ought not to be. Like being in a supermarket and you've paid for the things you've bought but for some reason it didn't occur to you to bag up your purchases as you